The Personality of Milton

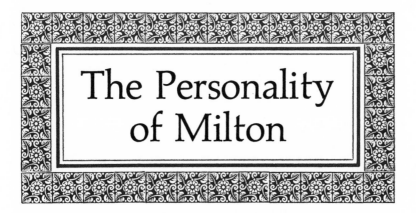

The Personality of Milton

Edward Wagenknecht

University of Oklahoma Press

Norman

RECENT BOOKS BY EDWARD WAGENKNECHT

Nathaniel Hawthorne, Man and Writer (New York, 1961)
Mark Twain: The Man and His Work (Norman, 1961, 1967)
Washington Irving: Moderation Displayed (New York, 1962)
The Movies in the Age of Innocence (Norman, 1962)
Edgar Allan Poe: The Man Behind the Legend (New York, 1963)
Chicago (Norman, 1964)
Seven Daughters of the Theater (Norman, 1964)
Harriet Beecher Stowe: The Known and the Unknown (New York, 1965)
Dickens and the Scandalmongers: Essays in Criticism (Norman, 1965)
The Man Charles Dickens: A Victorian Portrait (Norman, 1966)
Henry Wadsworth Longfellow: Portrait of an American Humanist
(New York, 1966)
Merely Players (Norman, 1966)
John Greenleaf Whittier, A Portrait in Paradox (New York, 1967)
The Personality of Chaucer (Norman, 1968)
As Far As Yesterday: Memories and Reflections (Norman, 1968)
The Supernaturalism of New England, by John Greenleaf Whittier,
edited E.W. (Norman, 1969)
William Dean Howells: The Friendly Eye (New York, 1969)
Marilyn Monroe: A Composite View, edited E.W. (Philadelphia, 1969)

The paper on which this book is printed bears the watermark of the University of Oklahoma Press and has an effective life of at least three hundred years.

INTERNATIONAL STANDARD BOOK NUMBER: 0-8061-0916-5

LIBRARY OF CONGRESS CATALOG CARD NUMBER: 71-108807

To my second grandson
Matthew James Wagenknecht
Son of David Arnold Wagenknecht
and Patricia Terwiliger Wagenknecht
Born at Brighton, Sussex, England
August 23, 1969

PREFACE

The Personality of Milton is a companion volume to *The Personality of Chaucer*, which was published by the University of Oklahoma Press in the spring of 1968. In due course, I hope it may be followed by "The Personality of Shakespeare," thus constituting a trilogy devoted to the three greatest English poets in their personal aspects.

So far as their self-revelation in their own works is concerned, Milton and Shakespeare stand at opposite extremes. Shakespeare was as purely the dramatic writer as it is possible for a human being to be,[1] while Milton created by dramatizing his own personality. Chaucer, as has been generally recognized, falls somewhere between the two. If with both Chaucer and Shakespeare the best materials for a character portrait must be derived from inferences, the student of Milton is always in danger of being overwhelmed by too much riches and of choosing the easiest way by accepting Milton's own estimate of himself uncritically. J. H.

---

[1] Milton might not wholly agree. Though he recognized the importance of distinguishing between dramatist and personae, he also believed that poets tend to put their own "sense" into the utterances of their best characters.

Hanford has said that Milton invites the world "to look at his work and his life together." He does more than invite. He insists. The self-isolating methods of the "New Criticism" are not for him or his work.

The classical statement of the differences between Milton and Shakespeare was made by Lowell long ago in *Among My Books*:

> Gentle as Milton's earlier portraits would seem to show him, he had in him by nature, or bred into him by fate, something of the haughty and defiant self-assertion of Dante and Michael Angelo. In no other English author is the man so large a part of his works. Milton's haughty conception of himself enters into all he says and does. Always the necessity of this one man became that of the whole human race for the moment. There were no walls so sacred but must go to the ground when *he* wanted elbow-room; and he wanted a great deal. Did Mary Powell, the cavalier's daughter, find the abode of a roundhead schoolmaster *incompatible* and leave it, forthwith the cry of the universe was for an easier dissolution of the marriage covenant. If *he* is blind, it is with excess of light, it is a divine partiality, an overshadowing with angels' wings. Phineus and Teiresias are admitted among the prophets because they, too, had lost their sight, and the blindness of Homer is of more account than his *Iliad*. After writing in rhyme till he was fifty, he finds it unsuitable for his epic, and it at once becomes "the invention of a barbarous age to set off wretched matter and lame metre." If the structure of *his* mind be undramatic, why, then, the English drama is naught, learned Jonson, sweetest Shakespeare and the rest notwithstanding, and he will compose a tragedy on the Greek model with the blinded Samson for its hero, and he will compose it partly in rhyme. Plainly he belongs to the intenser kind of men whose yesterdays are in no way responsible for their tomorrows. And this makes him perennially interesting even to those who hate his politics, despise his Socinianism, and find his greatest poem a bore. . . .

It results from the almost scornful withdrawal of Milton into the fortress of his absolute personality that no great poet is so uniformly self-conscious as he. We should say of Shakespeare that he had the power of transforming himself into everything; of Milton, that he had that of transforming everything into himself. Dante is individual rather than self-conscious, and he, the cast-iron man, grows pliable as a field of grain at the breath of Beatrice, and flows away in waves of sunshine. But Milton never lets himself go for a moment. As other poets are possessed by their theme, so is he *self*-possessed, his great theme being John Milton, and his great duty that of interpreter between him and the world. I say it with all respect, for he was well worthy translation, and it is out of Hebrew that the version is made. Pope says he makes God the Father reason "like a school-divine." The criticism is witty, but inaccurate. He makes Deity a mouthpiece for his present theology, and had the poem been written a few years later, the Almighty would have become more heterodox. Since Dante, no one has stood on these visiting terms with heaven.

Now it is precisely this audacity of self-reliance, I suspect, which goes far toward making the sublime, and which, falling by a hair's-breadth short thereof, makes the ridiculous. Puritanism showed both the strength and weakness of its prophetic nurture; enough of the latter to be scoffed out of England by the very men it had conquered in the field, enough of the former to intrench itself in three or four immortal memories. It has left an abiding mark in politics and religion, but its great monuments are the prose of Bunyan and the verse of Milton. It is a high inspiration to be the neighbor of great events; to have been a partaker in them, and to have seen noble purposes by their own self-confidence become the very means of ignoble ends, if it does not wholly repress, may kindle a passion of regret, deepening the song which dares not tell the reason of its sorrow. The grand loneliness of Milton in his later years, while it makes him the most attractive figure in our literary history, is reflected also in his maturer poems by a sublime independence of human sympathy like that with which mountains fascinate and rebuff us. But it is idle to talk of the loneliness of one the habitual companions of whose mind were the Past and the Future. I always seem to see him leaning in his blindness a hand on the shoulder of each, sure that the one will guard the song which the other had inspired.

Though it will not take the reader of this book long to discover that some of the details of Lowell's interpretation are open to serious question, the basic contrast developed is, I think, helpful for the understanding of both the poets under consideration.

Milton was probably the most learned of all the very great poets, and his vast intellectual scope creates insurmountable problems for anyone who does not share it—that is, for practically everybody. However greatly one may admire him, it is much harder to feel at home with him than with Chaucer, and very rarely can one feel that he has probed either his sources or his meanings to their utmost depths. It is easy to stand before the portrait of a great man and exclaim in wonder over his perfections, but that is not the way understanding is achieved. It is even easier to stand off and throw mud at the portrait. In Milton's case there have been plenty to do that in the twentieth century, but little of the mud seems to have stuck. It is not that, even now, Milton is a "popular" poet or seems in any danger of becoming one; he speaks for us hardly more than he spoke for the Restoration world in which he published his greatest poems. But he still finds the "fit audience . . . though few" which he looked for then, and no responsible reader today cares to march under Mutschmann's tattered banner, or Ezra Pound's, or T. S. Eliot's (if one might discover where it was really placed), or even under that of Denis Saurat in his more exuberant moments, nor would anybody care to go back to the iconoclasm of Blake and Shelley, who thought Milton was of the devil's party without knowing it. (Marjorie Nicolson is penetrating indeed when she wonders whether Shelley ever read the later books of *Paradise Lost* or stopped short at the end of Book II!)[2]

Though the study of Milton upon which this book is based has embraced many years, the book is not the work of a Milton specialist, nor do I claim to have made an original contribution to Milton scholarship; my concern is summary and interpretation. I quote the verse, by permission, from the Cambridge Edition of *The Complete Poetical Works of John Milton*, edited by Douglas Bush (Houghton Mifflin Company, 1965) and the prose from the Columbia Edition of Milton's *Works*; both publishers have been exceptionally kind and understanding. I owe a great debt to William Riley Parker's thirty years' study of Milton, summed up in his *Milton: A Biography* (Clarendon Press, 1968), which appeared just in time for me to make use of it and to lament the author's untimely death. Beyond this, I must allow my reader to judge my indebtedness from my footnotes, though I use these less to cite authorities than to refer the interested reader to more extensive discussion of particular points than I have room for. Of course I have made no attempt to list everything I have read, and of course I am not so foolish as to claim to have read everything that is relevant to my enormous subject. At one point or another, I am indebted to nearly all the important Milton scholars of the twentieth century, even when I disagree with them, and I can quote without altering a word what Edward S. LeComte wrote in the Preface to his *Yet Once More* (Liberal Arts Press, 1953):

indeed, I am sometimes in the ungracious position of mentioning very distinguished critics and scholars only to tilt with them

---

[2] On the anti-Miltonists, see Bernard Bergonzi, "Criticism and the Milton Controversy," in Frank Kermode, ed., *The Living Milton* (RKP, 1960), and the more popular but very entertaining account in Logan Pearsall Smith, *Milton and his Modern Critics* (LB, 1941). Bergonzi notes that the anti-Miltonists complain that their arguments have never been answered; admitting that they are, upon their own terms, unanswerable, he also finds that they are quite wrong because what they write does not "correspond with the facts . . . of literary experience. . . ." Patrick Murray takes a wider survey in *Milton, The Modern Phase, A Study of Twentieth Century Criticism* (BN, 1962).

on a particular point, which is—let me be the first to say—like the spoiled child who bites the hand that has fed him for years because on just one occasion or two, the food is not to his liking.

Finally I wish to express my gratitude to Professor Douglas Bush for his great kindness in reading my manuscript. Of course the responsibility for what I have written is mine alone.

EDWARD WAGENKNECHT

West Newton, Mass.

CONTENTS

xiii

The Personality of Milton

The following abbreviations are employed in the footnotes:

BN	Barnes & Noble
CE	*College English*
ColUP	Columbia University Press
CorUP	Cornell University Press
CW	Chatto & Windus
DP	Lincoln MacVeagh, The Dial Press
ELH	*English Literary History*
H	Harper & Brothers
HLQ	*Huntington Library Quarterly*
HTR	*Harvard Theological Review*
HUP	Harvard University Press
JEGP	*Journal of English and Germanic Philology*
JHI	*Journal of the History of Ideas*
JHP	Johns Hopkins Press
LB	Little, Brown & Company
M	The Macmillan Company
MLN	*Modern Language Notes*
MP	*Modern Philology*
OUP	Oxford University Press
PMLA	*Publications of the Modern Language Association*
PQ	*Philological Quarterly*
PUP	Princeton University Press
RES	*Review of English Studies*
RKP	Routledge and Kegan Paul
SP	*Studies in Philology*
SR	*Saturday Review*
UCP	The University of Chicago Press
UIP	The University of Illinois Press
UTQ	*University of Toronto Quarterly*

PROLOGUE:
YOUNG MILTON

Nearly seventy-five years ago, in a very interesting passage in his valuable study of Virgil, W. Y. Sellar tried to

express the dominant ethical or social characteristic—the ideal virtue or grace—or some of the great Roman writers by some word peculiarly expressive of Roman character or culture, and of frequent use in these writers themselves. Thus, in regard to Cicero . . . the word *humanitas* seems to sum up those qualities of heart and intellect which, in spite of the transparent weaknesses of his character, gained for him so much affection, and which, through the sympathy they enabled him to feel and arouse in others, were the secret of his unparalleled success as an advocate. To Lucretius we might apply the word *sanctitas*. . . . His own words *lepor* and *lepidus* express the graceful vivacity, artistic and social rather than ethical, which we associate with the thought of Catullus. The quality, mainly intellectual and social, but still not devoid of ethical content, of which Horace is the most perfect type is *urbanitas*. The full meaning of the great Roman word *gravitas* is only completely realized in the pages of Tacitus. And so it is only in Virgil . . . that we understand all the feelings of love to family and country, and of fidelity to the dead, and that sense of dependence upon a higher Power, sanctioning and sanctifying those feelings and the duties demanded by them, which the Romans comprehended in their use of the word *pietas*.[1]

If some careful student were to make the great English writers the subject of a similar exercise, John Milton might very well claim the word *austere* as his own. The world has been talking about "the young Catullus" for many years, and Chauncey Brewster Tinker called his book about Dr. Johnson's biographer *Young Boswell*, not because it deals essentially with the early years, but because he thought he saw in Boswell a certain essential immaturity which at once explained his more erratic behavior and at the same time illuminated the more winning capacity for hero worship without which he would not have been able to do the work which has kept his name in remembrance. Now surely nobody is in danger of thinking of Milton as essentially young, yet he was once quite as young as any of us. There is a story about a novelist who, when his publisher questioned his credentials for writing a book about children, replied haughtily, "*I* am a former child." Milton's credentials are even more convincing. In him austerity and a certain irrefragable innocence existed side by side. He carried many of his youthful characteristics into his mature years far more than most men do, and examining his youth is like listening to the overture of an opera by Wagner or Richard Strauss in which every leitmotif later to be developed is sounded.

William Vaughn Moody long ago reminded us that

in Milton's childhood Shakespeare was still alive, that at the Mermaid Tavern, probably in the very street where the scrivener's house[2] stood, Ben Jonson held his "merry meetings," and that most of the stalwart figures which had made the reign of the Virgin Queen illustrious were still to be seen about the streets of London. There was as yet hardly a hint of the passing

[1] *The Roman Poets of the Augustan Age: Virgil* (OUP, 1897), pp. 125–26.
[2] That is, the home of the Milton family.

4

away of those "spacious times," of the spirit of romance and adventure, which had filled Elizabethan England.

There is more than a hint of those "spacious times" in the work of young Milton, nor did their spirit ever wholly depart from him. We may not perhaps feel that Milton ever commanded the fierce Elizabethan zest with which a Kit Marlowe, for example, might embrace life, but his attitude was likewise alien to the moroseness with which the Puritan was soon to go about the world, as James Branch Cabell would say, like his father's representative in an alien country. Young Milton studied hard, rarely leaving his books before midnight, he tells us, from the time he was twelve years old, but he also led a sheltered life, comfortably cushioned against material want and fenced about with appreciation and understanding. The latter failed him upon his first encounter with Cambridge, from which he was apparently sent home after a dispute with his tutor. Though he was certainly not crushed by this contretemps, which was soon adjusted, Milton's amour propre must have felt the blow, and there is a faint air of overmuch protesting about the First Latin Elegy (to Charles Diodati) in which he proclaims his indifference to his plight: "If this be exile, to be again in the paternal home and free from cares, to follow pleasant diversions, then I do not refuse either the name or the fate of an outlaw and happily enjoy my state of banishment." Writing to his former tutor Thomas Young, now a pastor in Germany, he looks back lovingly to the days when "under his tutelage I first visited the retreats of Aonia and the hallowed glades of the twin-peaked mountain, and drained Pierian waters, and by Clio's favor I thrice wet my happy lips with Castalian wine." Young Milton, like all the bright young men in those days, was steeped in classical learning; we learn far more about what he was like in his youth from his Latin poems than from those he wrote in his native language; when he really wished to express what lay close to his heart he turned to the alien tongue. He was not deficient in animal spirits either; he had a particular fondness for Ovid (which he was never to lose), and he found his Muse quickened by the com-

5

ing of spring. "Mother earth, refreshed, puts on her brief youth, and now, loosened from frost, the ground turns green and sweet. Am I deceived, or is my power of song also returning, and has inspiration come to me through the bounty of spring?" And though the subject is stock, I think we may feel that personal enthusiasm for life and living shows through the "Naturam non pati senium," in which he argues against the view that the power of nature wanes with time.

All this seems more humanistic than Puritan. The tribute to Shakespeare (Milton's first English poem to be published) was much in the spirit of Ben Jonson's tribute; in his sonnet to the nightingale he professed himself dedicated to love and poetry:

> Whether the Muse or Love call thee his mate,
> Both them I serve, and of their train am I.

The well-known passage in "L'Allegro"—

> Then to the well-trod stage anon,
> If Jonson's learned sock be on,
> Or sweetest Shakespeare, Fancy's child,
> Warble his native wood-notes wild;

—and the reference to "the splendor of the curved theatre" in the First Latin Elegy do not stand alone to testify to his interest in an institution around whose portals many Puritans fancied they sniffed brimstone. But the lofty idealism we associate with Milton was already present. "At a Solemn[3] Music" shows that as early as 1633 he was convinced that neither music nor poetry could stand alone but that both must be consecrated to God's service.

Milton in his maturity was no celibate but a much-married man who poured scorn upon the hypocrites who defame as impure what God calls pure. But in youth it is clear that he kept his distance from women. In the Seventh Latin Elegy we learn that Cupid repaid his customary scorn by causing the poet to fall in love with a girl whom he saw on the streets of London, but there

[3] Sacred.

is no sense in taking this seriously. Girl-watching was nothing new for Milton; even the First Elegy speaks of the girls in the park—"stars that breathe out tempting flames" and "alluring cheeks that make pallid the crimson of the hyacinth and the glow of even your flower, Adonis!" But "while the indulgence of the blind boy permits," he must still prepare "to depart with all speed from this fortunate city and, with the help of divine moly, to keep far from the infamous halls of the treacherous Circe"; even "the rushy fens of the Cam" and "the hoarse murmur of the class-room" were better than such dangers! Milton's Italian love sonnets contain many conventional avowals of affection, but even here he avoids sensuality, explaining to Diodati that it is not "golden hair or a rosy cheek" which enthrall him, "but a foreign beauty of a new pattern rejoices my heart—proud modesty of bearing, in her eyes that clear sheen of lovely black, speech adorned by more than one language, and a gift of song that might well drive the laboring moon astray in the middle of the sky. . . ." In view of what we have now learned about Milton's interest in an Italian girl named Emilia, Moody may have exaggerated somewhat when he said that the young man's chief concern in his love poems (all written in foreign languages) was "to avoid the pitfalls of solecism," but all in all he was not far wrong.

As to social relations with members of his own sex, Milton was an emotional man—and boy—and he relished assurance of his worth, but for that side of sociality which means frivolity or dissipation, or even mere innocent trifling, he had little time or capacity. At home he had obviously been treated as a person of consideration from his birth and reared without the necessity upon his part of any painful accommodation. This does not seem to have handicapped him at St. Paul's School, where he made close friends of both Alexander Gill, Jr., and Charles Diodati, son of a London physician of Italian origin, whose temperament seems to have been somewhat sunnier than his own. At Cambridge it was different. Here his strict morals would have alone sufficed to erect a barrier between him and many of the other students, who dubbed him, to his disgust, "the Lady of Christ's," and, as has

7

already been noted, he had a disagreement with his first tutor, William Chappell. Not long absent from Cambridge, he was reassigned to Nathaniel Tovey, which, since such transfers were not the custom at Cambridge, may indicate that the authorities judged Chappell to have been unreasonable.

Certainly the capacity for admiration was not lacking in Milton; it was not for nothing that, in *Paradise Lost*, he was to nail down a fatal disability of the fallen angels in their incapacity for worship. To Thomas Young he writes in 1627 of "that most vehement desire after you which I feel makes me always fancy you with me, and speak to you and behold you as if you were present, and so (as generally happens in love) soothe my grief by a certain vain imagination of your presence." Yet even the long Latin poem which he sent to his father probably about 1631–32, and which constitutes a kind of apologia for his life up to this point, is as independent as it is grateful and affectionate. The young man boldly claims further leisure to prosecute his studies in his own way, and though there has obviously been some disagreement between his father and himself, both as to poetry in general and his own poetic career in particular, he maintains his position and corrects his father where he thinks him wrong. He simply would not enter into "the broad way" of commercial life, "where money slides more easily into the hand, and the golden hope of piling up wealth shines bright and sure," nor did he care to condemn his ears to the "noisy stupidity" of the courts, where "ill-guarded statutes" were aired. For he was "now one among the learned band, however low my place, and . . . [would] sit with a young victor's ivy and laurel."

He was always conscious that he belonged to a great community. Thus he does his best to make the great Manso realize that he comes from "no uncultivated race worthless to Apollo," and his interest in the girls of London seems inspired by patriotism as much as passion. "The prime glory belongs to British maidens; let it be enough for you, foreign women, to have second place." But, like all good patriots, Milton is indignant when his country

8

does something unworthy of her best self. Shame overcomes him when he remembers that Thomas Young must live in exile.

Native country, harsh parent, more cruel than the white rocks that are beaten by the foaming waves of your coast, is it right for you thus to expose your innocent children? Do you thus without pity force them away to an alien soil, do you allow them to go to far lands in quest of subsistence, men whom God's providence has sent to you, who bear the joyful tidings from heaven, and who teach the way that after death leads to the stars?

And in *Comus* we have a passionate plea for social justice, based on a more equable division of the world's goods, which has not yet been heeded and which sounds the more stridently in such an aristocratic form of diversion as the masque:

> "If every just man that now pines with want
> Had but a moderate and beseeming share
> Of that which lewdly pampered luxury
> Now heaps upon some few with vast excess,
> Nature's full blessings would be well dispensed
> In unsuperfluous even proportion,
> And she no whit encumbered of her store;
> And then the Giver would be better thanked,
> His praise due paid, for swinish gluttony
> Ne'er looks to Heav'n amidst his gorgeous feast,
> But with besotted base ingratitude
> Crams, and blasphemes his Feeder."

The strength and sturdiness that were to distinguish Milton the man were, therefore, already conspicuous in the youth. In this same *Comus*, take the calm confidence of the Elder Brother that

> Virtue may be assailed but never hurt.

It will not do to object that the sentiment is vitiated by being placed in the mouth of an unbelievably priggish character, for though this may be our reaction as we read, nobody believes that this is what Milton intended (the whole course of the fable justifies the Brother's faith). Moral idealism is closely allied to religion—for those reared in the English tradition at any rate—and piety might almost have been expected as a matter of course in a seventeenth century Englishman reared as Milton had been reared.

Milton did not keep either his idealism or his religion out of his poetry. Sending his Fourth Elegy to Thomas Young, he did wonder whether, in the midst of his battles, that soldier of the church could find time for the gentle muses, and it is clear that hours of questioning came to him, as they do to all of us, when he wondered what good it could do

> To tend the homely slighted shepherd's trade,
> And strictly meditate the thankless Muse?
> Were it not better done as others use,
> To sport with Amaryllis in the shade,
> Or with the tangles of Neaera's hair?

But he was never really tempted, any more than Christ could have been tempted in *Paradise Regained* by Belial's inept plan to "set women in his eye and in his walk." It was not so much that Neaera's hair did not attract him—or Amaryllis either—as that other incompatible things attracted him more. For even in these early days he was conscious of the infinite implications of human action, and resolved to live, as he expressed it in the noble sonnet now thought to have been written on his twenty-fourth birthday,

> As ever in my great Task-Master's eye.

Milton gives us his most considered view of all these matters in the Sixth Latin Elegy to Charles Diodati. It is not unfortunate that he should here admit that wine and dancing are useful sources of inspiration for *some* kinds of poetry, for the admission both saves him from the defect of weak priggishness and lends the force of climax to what follows. "Light elegy has the patronage of many gods and calls whom she will to her measure." But "if you would like to know what I am doing . . . I am singing the prince of peace, the son of Heaven, and the blessed ages promised in the sacred books." For such a poet only high thinking and plain living will do. "And his youth must be free from evil, and chaste, and his character upright, his hand without stain. . . . For the true poet is sacred to the gods, he is a priest of the gods; and his inmost soul and his lips breathe out Jove." The reference to "the prince of peace, the son of Heaven" indicates, of course, the ode "On the Morning of Christ's Nativity," and if creeds are to be judged by the fruits they produce, then Milton was right, for it is here that we first encounter his authentic voice.

> Nature in awe to him
> Had doffed her gaudy trim,
>   With her great Maker so to sympathize;
> It was no season then for her
> To wanton with the sun, her lusty paramour.

All this, it goes without saying, is the idealism of a young man, but, as we shall see, unlike most men, Milton did not forget the dreams of youth amid the disillusionment of maturity. "He who would write well hereafter in laudable things ought himself to be a true poem." Put that statement beside the dictum of a young man of the nineteenth century—Oscar Wilde's pronunciemento that the value of an idea has nothing whatever to do with the sincerity of the man who expresses it. The everlasting clean-cut distinction between the doer of the Word and the mere sayer thereof could hardly be more succinctly displayed.

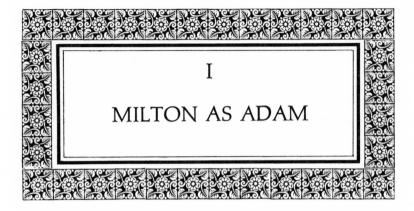

I

MILTON AS ADAM

The most affecting passages in *Paradise Lost* are personal allusions, and when we are fairly in Eden, Adam and Milton are often difficult to be separated.

Emerson's essay on Milton

I

In the Morgan Library portrait of Milton at the age of ten, Parker rightly finds "a delicate, rather wistful face, . . . pink and white complexion, . . . inquiring eyes, . . . [and] closely cropped auburn hair." The Onslow portrait in the National Portrait Gallery, painted while he was a student at Cambridge, shows the teen-ager this child developed into. His third wife, who outlived him, liked it better than any of the pictures published in his books, which she said were not at all like him, and his daughter Deborah was to admire the Faithorne drawing but not the harsh engraving made from it. The face was heart-shaped; the eyes have been described as "brown" and again as "slate-grey." Deborah called the hair "brown" and "lank" (Aubrey says, marginally, "abrown"), and the complexion "fair," with "a little red in his cheeks," which may well be what the anonymous biographer means by "ruddy" or Milton himself by his statement that he was "the reverse of bloodless or pallid." Aubrey says further that he was of medium height (which probably indicated a somewhat lower stature in the seventeenth century than it does today), and that his "beautiful and well proportioned body" furnished a fitting tenement for his "harmonical and ingenious soul," and Wood adds that "his deportment was affable, his gait erect and manly, bespeaking courage and undauntedness." With him as with the rest of us these gifts were the sport of time, and Jonathan Richardson strikes a wryly amusing note when he says that in later life Milton was "not short and thick, but he would have been so, had he been somewhat shorter and thicker than he was"! It is interesting that the great Italian nobleman Manso agreed with Milton's English admirers as to his multitudinous perfections, finding the only flaw in his (from Manso's point of view) heretical religious views.

> Mind, form, grace, face, and morals are perfect;
>   but if thy creed were,
> Then not Anglic alone, truly angelic thoud'st be.

Milton did not often find it necessary to discuss his appearance in print, but in *The Second Defense of the People of England*, he set out to confound an enemy who had described him as "a monster horrid, ugly, huge, and blind" and, at the same time, "lean, bloodless, and shrivelled"! He had never expected to enter a beauty contest against the Cyclops, but he did not wish those who did not know him to think of him as "some monster with a dog's head, or a rhinoceros." Admitting his short stature (but "why should that stature be called small which is large enough for every virtuous purpose?"), he denied his alleged paleness and declared himself quite unwrinkled and fully ten years younger in appearance than the forty years he carried. This was certainly true. Milton grew up slowly; both his early portraits look younger than he was when they were painted, and the famous Sonnet VII, apologizing for his slow productivity, grants that

Perhaps my semblance might deceive the truth,
That I to manhood am arrived so near.

But the pathetic thing about the apologia in the *Second Defense* is the innocent vanity Milton shows in relation to the only aspect of his blindness he could regard as fortunate, the fact that to "external appearance" his eyes were "as completely without injury, as clear and bright, without the semblance of a cloud, as the eyes of those whose sight is most perfect." And he adds, "In this respect only am I a dissembler; and here it is against my will."

His habits were those of a moderate man who took reasonable care of his health. In his middle years, he tells us, he was "up and stirring, in winter often ere the sound of the bell awake men to labor or to devotion, in summer oft with the bird that first rouses, or not much tardier, to read good authors, or cause them to be read, till the attention be weary or memory have his full fraught." After the Restoration, when he was blind, he went to bed about nine and was often awake as early as half past four, when the Hebrew Bible would be read to him. He ate sparingly but was far from indifferent to the quality of his food, as the enticing description of the vegetarian banquet which Eve served to Raphael (they "sufficed," not "burdened," nature) must show, and he seems to have relished the culinary skill of his third wife "Betty" (Elizabeth Minshull). His supper sometimes consisted only of "olives or some light thing," after which he seems to have relished a pipe and a glass of water. Only "inoffensive must" is drunk in Eden; intoxication does not enter human experience until after the fall, when the conduct of both Adam and Eve is described in terms of a libidinous, drunken orgy. With Eden lost, the craving for strong drink powerfully increases man's woes.

"Some, as thou saw'st, by violent stroke shall die,
By fire, flood, famine; by intemperance more
In meats and drinks, which on the earth shall bring

Diseases dire, of which a monstrous crew
Before thee shall appear, that thou may'st know
What misery th'inabstinence of Eve
Shall bring on men."

There is another temperance sermon in *Samson Agonistes*:

"O madness, to think use of strongest wines
And strongest drinks our chief support of health,
When God with these forbidd'n made choice to rear
His mighty champion, strong above compare,
Whose drink was only from the liquid brook."

Milton himself eschewed liquor, though he drank wine, sparingly, and rarely between meals. Dr. Johnson noted that "no part of 'L'Allegro' is made to arise from the pleasures of the bottle." Wine is included in the hospitality promised to Edward Lawrence in Sonnet XX, but it is not emphasized, and, as Marjorie Nicolson has remarked, it plays a much less important role than in the corresponding piece by Ben Jonson.[1]

---

[1] There is a very suggestive passage at the end of the exposition of Deuteronomy 24:1-2 in *Tetrachordon*:

What more foul and common sin among us than drunkenness, and who can be ignorant that if the importation of wine, and the use of all strong drink were forbid, it would both clean rid the possibility of commiting that odious vice, and men might afterwards live happily and healthfully, without the use of those intoxicating liquors. Yet who is there the severest of them all, that ever propounded to lose his sack, his ale, toward the certain abolishment of so great a sin, who is there of them, the holiest, that less loves his rich Canary at meals, though it be fetched from places that hazard the religion of them who fetch it, and though it make his neighbor drink out of the same tun? While they forbid not therefore the use of that liquid merchandise, which forbidden would utterly remove a most loathsome sin, and not impair either the health or the refreshment of mankind, supplied in many other ways, why do they forbid a law of God, the forbidding whereof brings into an excessive bondage, oft times the best of men, and betters not the worse? He to remove a national vice, will not pardon his cups, nor think it concerns him to forbear the quaffing of that outlandish grape in his unnecessary fulness, though other men abuse it ever so much, nor is he so abstemious as to intercede with the magistrate that all manner of drunkenness be banished the Commonwealth, and yet for the fear of a less inconvenience unpardonably requires of his brethern, in their extreme necessity, to debar themselves the use of God's permissive law, though it might be their saving and no

15

Milton was trained in fencing and wrestling, and as a schoolmaster he saw that his pupils were thus trained also. After he went blind he exercised on a kind of swing, and remained a great walker, sometimes staying out three or four hours at a stretch. Personally I do not believe that great walkers are, generally speaking, sports-minded people, and I believe Milton exercised because he desired physical fitness and not because he enjoyed the exercise itself. In *Paradise Lost* only the least exalted of the fallen angels, newly arrived in hell, turn to athletics; the others occupy themselves with artistic matters or with philosophical discourse. But however all this may be, two of the most intimate glimpses we have of Milton come from Jonathan Richardson, who tells us both that "he used to sit in a grey coarse cloth coat at the door of his house, near Bunhill Fields, without Moorgate, in warm, sunny weather, to enjoy the fresh air" and that he liked to dictate "leaning backward obliquely in an easy chair, with his leg flung over the elbow of it."

His two great physical afflictions were blindness and, in his last years, gout, which marked his hands with chalkstones and caused him to say that without this his blindness would be tolerable. Though he was sparing in his use of physic, his health was never robust; as he tells us in the *Second Defense*, he was "always stronger in mind than in body." I, for one, cannot bear even to read about the "remedies" to which he submitted himself when he was losing his sight; I do not dare to think what it must have been to endure them.[2]

His gout he resented as a peculiar injustice, for in his day it was regarded as the peculiar scourge of drunkards. Towards his blind-

---

man's endangering the more. Thus this peremptory strictness we may discern of what sort it is, how unequal and how unjust.

In its context, this cannot be called a plea for prohibition, but I agree with Masson that there is a certain sympathy with prohibition in its tone though not in its argument. If prohibition is impracticable, Milton seems to be saying, it is the foolishness and selfishness of mankind which makes it so; a truly rational commonwealth would surely permit no traffic in wines and liquors.

[2] Cf. Parker, p. 992; James Holly Hanford, *John Milton, Poet and Humanist* (The Press of Western Reserve University, 1966), pp. 198–99. Parker notes that, unlike Shakespeare, Milton never ridicules physicians.

ness he would seem to have taken up, at one time or another, almost every conceivable attitude. In 1654 he described his symptoms in some detail in a letter to Leonard Philaris, and these and other data have served a variety of commentators for a variety of diagnoses, both sane and insane.[3] His sight was beginning to fail at least as early as 1644. The left eye went first, and by the winter of 1651–52 he was wholly blind. Much has been said about the strain he put upon his eyes by his intemperate study from boyhood, and he himself thought he had sacrificed his eyesight to write his *Defense of the People of England*. These things can hardly have helped, but Milton's defect was probably congenital, and it seems unlikely that anything could have saved him, at least in the state of medical knowledge and practice which prevailed in the seventeenth century. "To be blind is not miserable; not to be able to bear blindness, that is miserable." In the *Second Defense* he refutes the cruel charge of his enemies that his sufferings were punishment for sin by calling the roll of the illustrious blind, making his virtue an affliction and a consecration. "Woe be to him who makes a mock of us; woe be to him who injures us; he deserves to be devoted to the public curse." Nor did he ever doubt that the cause for which he had, as he thought of it, made the sacrifice was worthy of all he had paid. "Why, in truth," he wrote the French scholar Emeric Bigot, "should I not bear gently the deprivation of sight, when I may hope that it is not so much lost as revoked and retracted inwards, for the sharpening rather than the blunting of my mental edge?" In a way, he had always known that that was the way it would be, for in *Comus* he had made the Elder Brother declare:

> "Virtue could see to do what Virtue would
> By her own radiant light, though sun and moon
> Were in the flat sea sunk."

By the time he wrote *Paradise Lost* he had passed beyond theory to experience in these matters,

[3] See Parker's summary, p. 988, n. 133. The fullest study is Eleanor G. Brown, *Milton's Blindness* (ColUP, 1934).

> though fall'n on evil days,
> On evil days though fall'n, and evil tongues;
> In darkness, and with dangers compassed round,
> And solitude.

The seasons still kept their course,

> but not to me returns
> Day, or the sweet approach of ev'n or morn,
> Or sight of vernal bloom, or summer's rose,
> Or flocks, or herds, or human face divine;
> But cloud instead, and ever-during dark
> Surrounds me, from the cheerful ways of men
> Cut off....

For though man is a spiritual being, made in the image of his Father, he is not and cannot be all spirit while he inhabits the flesh, nor was Milton ever fanatic enough to think so. It is nonsense to suppose that he meant Samson as an image of himself, but if he wrote *Samson Agonistes* after losing his sight, it is equally silly to suppose that he was unaware of the very personal, poignant meaning which some of Samson's utterances had for him.

> "O loss of sight, of thee I most complain!
> Blind among enemies, O worse than chains,
> Dungeon, or beggary, or decrepit age!
> Light, the prime work of God, to me is extinct,
> And all her various objects of delight
> Annulled, which might in part my grief have eased,
> Inferior to the vilest now become
> Of man or worm; the vilest here excel me,
> They creep, yet see; I, dark in light exposed
> To daily fraud, contempt, abuse and wrong,
> Within doors, or without, still as a fool,
> In power of others; never in my own;
> Scarce half I seem to live, dead more than half.

O dark, dark, dark, amid the blaze of noon,
Irrecoverably dark, total eclipse
Without all hope of day!"

II

Though Milton was a great optimist, he had comparatively little humor, and he acknowledged that his "faculty" in "festivities and jests" was "very slight." He granted laughter "strong and sinewy force in teaching," but the mere fact that he couples it with anger as the "two most rational faculties of human intellect" alone shows that he was no true comic spirit.[4] For all that, he had more humor than the casual reader today always recognizes, and indeed much of it is lost without specialized knowledge. Dora Raymond writes of his college disputations and exercises:

Sometimes the lad appealed pathetically to the muses to deliver him from his ungrateful tasks. Sometimes he prefaced the brief matter of his disquisitions with lengthy introductions on subjects better to his liking,—the decline and fall of the Roman Empire or the events of high Olympus. He treated bewildering subjects in a manner purposely bewildering. He acknowledged that, whether or not he seemed so to his reader, to himself he was a great bore. At times he concluded his conscious imbecilities with accommodations of the invincibility of truth, which was so shamefully obscured by the vain foam of words of schoolmen and their suffering pupils.[5]

Readers of Mark Twain may not find any of this very spontaneous, but that was not what Milton's learned, highly Latinate audience required. The humor in the letters to Diodati is easier to grasp; so are the quips in the second of the two poems upon the death of the apparently somewhat curmudgeonly Cambridge Uni-

---

[4] Cf. Voltaire's "Laughter arises from a gaiety of disposition, absolutely incompatible with contempt and indignation."

[5] *Oliver's Secretary: John Milton in an Era of Revolt* (Minton, Balch, 1932). See also " 'Or o're the tiles,' A Note on Milton's Humor," in Alden Sampson, *Studies in Milton and an Essay on Poetry* (Moffat, Yard, 1913); cf. his Postscript to "Milton's Private Correspondence," p. 136.

versity carrier Hobson (to whom we owe the phrase "Hobson's choice"). Some may object that as obituary notices both these poems are somewhat heartless, yet the first ends on as tender a note as one could require under the circumstances:

> If any ask for him, it shall be said,
> "Hobson has supped, and's newly gone to bed."

The later sonnet to a Royalist commander, promising him a true Elizabethan immortality through poetry, would he only spare the poet's dwelling "when the attack was intended to the city" in 1642, seems a little coy and self-conscious to many modern readers, but much of this feeling is due to the quite unnecessary assumption that it was intended to be posted at Milton's door.

The most self-conscious bit of humor in *Paradise Lost* occurs when Eve prepares her vegetarian feast for Raphael in Book V— "No fear lest dinner cool." Tennyson called this "terrible bathos," but the objection comes with little force from the poet who ended "Enoch Arden" with the hero's "costly" funeral and spoiled a beautiful passage in "A Dream of Fair Women" by including a reference to the quite unpoetic and wholly irrelevant fact that the roots of the "green plant" in the garden crept "to the garden water-pipes beneath."[6] If Satan was intended to be as much of an "ass" as C. S. Lewis found him, there are also examples of cosmic, gigantic humor in *Paradise Lost* ("he that sitteth in the heavens shall laugh"), perhaps even in the futile, large-scale destructiveness of the rebel angels, turning vainly against the Father in a war which, like nuclear war in the twentieth century, cannot be won. But though Milton believed that scornful laughter had its proper place in controversy, this is hardly what most of us mean by humor, and Masson may well have been right when he quoted "Being Religious by Deputy: or the Use of a Popular London Clergyman" as "the richest bit of humor I have yet found in Mil-

---

[6] The countryman in Mrs. Gaskell's *Cranford* decided that Tennyson was a great poet when he discovered that Tennyson knew ashbuds are black in March. As Paul Elmer More has conveniently pointed out, it would have been more to the point, on the data supplied, to decide that he was a good botanist.

ton, and . . . better and deeper, in that kind, than anything in Sydney Smith."[7]

Humor can exist without optimism of course and, by the same token, optimism without humor. The Elder Brother in *Comus* (to quote him once more) is certainly not a humorist, but he declares that

> "where an equal poise of hope and fear
> Does arbitrate the event, my nature is
> That I incline to hope rather than fear,
> And gladly banish squint suspicion."

And in this respect he truly mirrored the temperament of his creator.

Milton supported Cromwell's government as a step toward the regeneration of mankind and the establishment of a utopia among men. He wrote his ecclesiastical and divorce pamphlets as a means of delivering men from churchly and domestic tyranny, and then, when Mary Powell came back to him in search of reconciliation, he showed his optimism again in a totally different way by accepting her and trying marriage once more in spite of everything he had written about the miseries of a hopeless mismating. The *Ready and Easy Way* appeared when almost everybody else was about ready to grant that the great experiment had failed and that there was nothing for it now but to return to monarchy. "In doubtful postures of our affairs," Milton once declared, "my mind never betrayed any symptom of despondence, nor was I more afraid than became me of malice or even of death."

Of course he cannot possibly have believed that the suggestions he made in the Commonwealth pamphlet would be accepted. What he did believe was that a man must continue trying until the door is finally and absolutely closed. "An idle ease has never

---

[7] "He entertains him, gives him gifts, feasts him, lodges him; his Religion comes home at night, prays, is liberally supped and sumptuously laid to sleep, rises, is saluted; and after the malmsey or some well-spiced brewage, and better breakfasted than he whose morning appetite would have gladly fed on green figs between Bethany and Jerusalem, his Religion walks abroad at eight, and leaves his kind entertainer in the shop, trading all day without his Religion."

had any charm for me." This is perhaps what Tillyard meant by seeing Milton as "the perpetual monument of the pioneering spirit in man" and "the only man of this type who has translated his mental urge into literature and not into action."[8] Moody called his imagination roccoco; recently it has more often been denominated baroque. Whatever you call it, there can be no doubt that it is there. Tillyard has compared Milton with Rubens and with Blake's "I want, I want."[9] If Charles Wesley could not see why the devil should have all the good tunes, Milton was not willing to leave energy and fertility in the hands of Comus and his party. As Helen Gardner has written,

> The seventh is the one purely happy book of *Paradise Lost* and shows Milton's genius at its most genial and delightful, filling out the bare narrative of Genesis with a wealth of knowledge and imagination, with constant touches of observation, of beauty, humour, delicacy, and grotesqueness. It is inspired by Milton's passionate belief in the goodness of the natural world as it was created and his delight in the principle of life in all its manifestations.[10]

Dame Helen also calls attention to his sparing use of horror, even in hell; in this respect he was far less material than Dante. Of late years it has often been pointed out that he has no suggestion of what it is now fashionable to call "cosmic horror" and that the vast spaces of Infinitude hold no terrors for him.

Yet this is the same Milton who caused Michael to advise Adam:

"Nor love thy life, nor hate; but what thou liv'st
Live well, how long or short permit to Heav'n."

And this may help us to understand how this Milton, who had so much romantic feeling, avoided all the romantic absurdities. His faith was such that, like Dante's, his ultimate vision of life was

[8] E. M. W. Tillyard, *Milton* (DP, 1930), p. 368.
[9] *The Miltonic Setting* (Cambridge University Press, 1938), p. 70; cf. p. 69.
[10] *A Reading of Paradise Lost* (OUP, 1965), p. 75. See, especially, ll. 463 ff., on the animals, and the cosmic dance in ll. 557 ff.

"comic," not tragic, but he never underestimated the forces in human nature and in the universe itself which stand opposed to both human welfare and God's will; in this respect he is a truly realistic writer. After the Restoration, when England had suffered a political fall, he was forced to give up his hope of regeneration through political action, but instead of despair, the result was a shift to

"A paradise within thee, happier far."[11]

But even then he was no solipsist. The impression of mellow good humor which he gave out was stronger than ever during his last years; despite his political disappointment, blindness, and sometimes racking pain, he was "very merry," "of a cheerful humor," and "delightful company"—with such phrases are the records studded.

The ending of *Paradise Lost* has been much discussed. Many eighteenth-century critics thought it was not happy enough for an epic, and Richard Bentley, the great classical scholar, who made such a glorious fool of himself by treating the text as if it were something that had come down from antiquity, proposed amending the last two lines to

Then hand in hand, with *social* steps their way
Through Eden took, *with heavenly comfort cheer'd*.

The problem of the "fortunate fall" in *Paradise Lost* must be discussed elsewhere in these pages; here let it suffice to say that though Milton sees God as ultimately victorious in His own world, his *immediate* outlook, as communicated to Adam, is far from rosy. If his "faith is strong," yet "his hope is remote." He

has been through the war, and seen his own and others' high expectations defeated and their reforms thwarted, the righteous man put down and the wicked exalted in his place. His eye hath kept watch o'er man's mortality, and man's frailty as well. But his faith does not waver, his hope is not quenched. His spirit is

[11] See G. C. Taylor, *PQ*, XXVIII (1949), 208, for the possible influence here of Robert Crofts, *A Paradise Within Us or the Happie Mind* (1640).

23

steadfast, not bent upon the glorious but vain and fleeting shows of their world, like that of a humanist, but raised above them.[12]

III

In days gone by, it was the fashion to think of Milton as a key man in Cromwell's government; he was never that. He looked after foreign correspondence; he used his pen to justify government courses; but there is no reason to suppose that he ever really influenced policy. Henry James once remarked that "the only form of riot or revel ever known to . . . [himself was] that of the visiting mind." Milton could never have expressed it that way; for one thing, his social conscience would not have permitted it. But he did not need to wait for later years to learn that the paradise within is fairer and the world within more interesting than those that lie outside. Power as he thought of it was that of the thinker or creator, and the only rule that could possibly have interested him must have been the rule of men's minds. He was a poet born, and he loved beauty. Moreover he was the kind of poet whose successful functioning demands a foundation of vast learning. And all this led him into the ways of a vast and varied exploring of the world within.

It might seem to be pointing to the world without in the first instance, for the lover of beauty is likely to encounter her first in nature. In Milton's case this is perhaps only partially true, for many of his references to nature have a literary flavor. Parker, for example, calls the Fifth Latin Elegy "an English spring glimpsed through the window of Ovid" and "April felt in a study." Much of Milton's nature imagery is generalized and conventionalized to such an extent that it is often impossible to tell what came from nature and what from books. The

Mountains on whose barren breast
The laboring clouds do often rest

12 Elmer Edgar Stoll, "Milton, Puritan of the Seventeenth Century," in *Poets and Playwrights* (University of Minnesota Press, 1930). See also his "Milton a Romantic," in *From Shakespeare to Joyce* (Doubleday, 1944).

of "L'Allegro" antedated his ever having seen a mountain. He saw the Alps when he went to Italy, and though many have conjectured their influence upon the landscapes of *Paradise Lost* he never speaks of them as such. The birds in the nightingale sonnet are literary and conventional; so, of course, are the wonderful little vignette of the whale in *Paradise Lost* (I, 200–208), the thunderclouds (II, 714–18), and the coming of evening (IV, 598–609) and of morn (V, 136–43). But this is not the whole story. Parker finds the true spirit of the English countryside in "On a May Morning," describing it as "the first of Milton's poems which praises natural beauty seen outside of books." I should say that more actual observation appears in the reference to the careless uprooting of the carnation by the "unheedy swain" in "An Epitaph on the Marchioness of Winchester" than by anything in the "May Morning," and the Seventh Prolusion speaks of the "woods and streams" and "beloved village elms" of a rapturous summer in the country. The barnyard scene in "L'Allegro" may have been suggested by Chaucer, but surely Milton must have witnessed it too, as well as having heard the hounds and horn which immediately follow. Of course he had seen "the wandering moon" of "Il Penseroso" too, and surely he must have observed the "minute drops from off the eaves" as well as the morning dew on the leaves and flowers of which he speaks in *Paradise Lost* (V, 747–48). I should also say that he certainly must have seen the

> autumnal leaves that strow the brooks
> In Vallombrosa

(I, 302–303), and one of Miss Nicolson's most exciting articles argues that he actually saw something of his hell in the volcanic phenomena observed in the Phlegraean fields near Naples.[13]

The most interesting mention of animals is in the *Christian*

---

[13] Marjorie H. Nicolson, "Milton's Hell and the Phlegraean Fields," *UTQ*, VII (1938), 500–13. Mark Pattison, *Milton* (H, 1880), pp. 23–27, formulates an inconclusive case against Milton's being a close observer of nature. But see further Tillyard's "Milton's Visual Imagination," in his *The Miltonic Setting*. B. A. Wright, *Milton's* Paradise Lost (BN, 1962), Ch. V, refutes the view that Milton is vague in his nature references because of defective eyesight.

Doctrine, where Milton goes out of his way to insist upon their being treated with compassion, but I find no references to his keeping pets, and I have no idea how much animals meant to him personally. He had certainly watched and meditated upon the flight of birds (*Paradise Lost,* VII, 425–30), and I should say that he had probably watched the swarming of bees also (I, 768–71).[14] The most prominent animal in *Paradise Lost* is obviously the predetermined serpent, but his is purely a passive role, for Milton follows the Augustine-Calvin "line" of a devil-possessed snake, and this is one of the points where he is obviously plot-ridden to his disadvantage. In Genesis the serpent is a folklore animal who himself takes the initiative in deceiving Eve, and the doom pronounced upon him is therefore just, but in *Paradise Lost* it is unjust, for he did not act at all. The devil, who possessed himself of his body without his acquiescence, acted *through* him, and he was cursed for nothing worse than having been victimized. "Milton does not know why the serpent was cursed," writes Northrop Frye, "and it is characteristic of a curious flat-footed honesty in Milton's mind that he should spread so obvious a bewilderment over a dozen lines of blank verse."

Did Milton, then, "love" nature? In the Romantic sense in which we now use the term, I am not sure it applies to a seventeenth-century writer, but what "garden poet" would you exchange for Milton? His Eden has many theological and literary sources; it is neither a formal garden nor an architectural garden but a "landscape garden," presenting "nature in miniature," and it shows the influence of the controversies current in the seventeenth century as to whether gardens should be "regular" or "irregular."[15] We know that Milton himself was fond of gardens,

---

[14] For Milton's use of animal imagery, see James Whaler, "Animal Simile in *Paradise Lost,*" PMLA, XLVII (1932), 534–53; F. Manley, MLN, LXXVI (1961), 398–403; Allan F. Price, "Incidental Imagery in *Areopagitica,*" MP, XLIX (1952), 217–22. Mr. Price finds animal imagery in the *Areopagitica* negligible, but the most famous image in the pamphlet—"muing her mighty youth"—is animal, and this has occasioned much confusion and commentary; see R. S. Loomis, MLN, XXXII (1917), 437–38; G. U. Yule, RES, XIX (1943), 61–66; L. C. Martin, RES, XXI (1945), 44–46.

generally managed to have one of his own, and missed his garden when he had to go into hiding after the Restoration. As an educator, he did not expect students to study much during the spring, thinking it "an injury and sullenness against nature not to go out and see her riches, and partake in her rejoicing with heaven and earth."

The great Shakespeare scholar E. E. Stoll, who most resolutely worked up the case for Milton as a Romantic, found that "more than any poet before him he delights in a landscape desolate and solitary, or darkened with superstitious and legendary associations," though he promptly adds that Milton has "no hunger or thirst for the Infinite, in the right Romantic fashion; nor . . . any thought of communing with Nature, or worshipping her, like Wordsworth or Keats, or blending his being with her, like Shelley." But it was not "hunger or thirst for the Infinite" that Milton lacked; it was simply that he knew this could not be satisfied through anything finite, nor did he possess the kind of being which "blends" comfortably with anything. In his world only God was worthy of worship, and though Milton's God expressed himself through nature—

> "Adam, thou knowest heav'n his, and all the earth,
> Not this rock only; his omnipresence fills
> Land, sea, and air, and every kind that lives,
> Fomented by his virtual power and warmed"[16]

—He was never, like that of the pantheists, in danger of being swallowed up by it. Only Eve is stupid enough to worship a tree, and that is after the Fall, when it has undone her.

There can be no question about the "inwardness" of aesthetic appreciation. Milton is strangely silent about the paintings he must have seen in Italy, and though this has not prevented his commentators from discerning kinship between Renaissance art and his poems and speculating about the possible influence of

---

[15] See Helen Gardner, A Reading of Paradise Lost, p. 79; Marjorie Nicolson, John Milton: A Reader's Guide to his Poetry (Farrar, Straus, 1963), pp. 237-39.
[16] Paradise Lost, XI, 335-38; cf. V, 153 ff.

one upon the other, most of this is as conjectural as Miss Pope's guess that the closing scene of *Paradise Regained* could have been derived from some unidentified religious painting.[17] Architecture is a somewhat less elusive matter. When II Penseroso prays

> But let my due feet never fail
> To walk the studious cloister's pale,
> And love the high embowèd roof
> With antique pillars massy proof,
> And storied windows richly dight,
> Casting a dim religious light,

he would seem to be remembering old St. Paul's, and Miss Nicolson has now made it seem very likely that Pandemonium is St. Peter's and the council chamber attached to it the Vatican.[18] If she is right, then these are the subtlest and most deadly anti-Catholic passages Milton ever wrote.

Music was another matter altogether, and Milton resembles Browning as one of the few English poets whose enthusiasm is matched by his technical knowledge. His father, a scrivener by profession, was a composer by avocation and an associate of the most distinguished musicians of his time. He once received a medal for an elaborate composition presented to a foreign prince.[19] There was music in the Milton home, and the poet, who had "a delicate, tunable voice," was taught how to use it by his father. He himself wrote lyrics for music, and legend says he also composed. When he was living in the country after his Cambridge years, he would go to London from time to time to find what was new in music and in mathematics. Later he brought music books home from Italy. He used *tetrachordon*, a Greek musical term, as a title for one of his divorce pamphlets.

[17] Elizabeth Marie Pope, Paradise Regained: *The Tradition and the Poem* (JHP, 1947). Emile Saillens, *John Milton, Man, Poet, Polemist* (BN, 1964), speaks of Milton's silence concerning the Sistine Chapel but adds that "no travel diary of this period even mentions Raphael."

[18] *John Milton, A Reader's Guide*, pp. 196–98.

[19] See Sigmund Spaeth, *Milton's Knowledge of Music* (University of Michigan Press, 1936); Ernest Brennecke, Jr., *John Milton the Elder and his Music* (ColUP, 1938).

28

He gave the great American singer Geraldine Farrar a title for her autobiography when he wrote in "Arcades":

Such sweet compulsion doth in music lie,
To lull the daughters of Necessity.

Paradise Lost is bathed in music, which is associated with virtually everything that occurs in it. "Monody," which he applies to "Lycidas," was a musical term with specific denotation for Milton's contemporaries, and Gretchen Finney[20] finds close parallels between the structure of this poem and the Italian music drama and oratorio, specifically the Orfeo operas of Monteverdi and Stefano Landi. In both the Nativity ode and "At a Solemn Music" Milton uses music as a symbol of moral perfection (harmony is righteousness and discord sin). He may have gone along with Shakespeare's dim view of the unmusical man,[21] for he believed music to have a beneficent influence upon man's moral nature, and in *Paradise Regained* (IV, 441–44) he attributed musical sensibility to Christ himself, which was well, for he could hardly have felt at home in heaven—Milton's heaven at any rate—without it.

As a teacher, Milton both taught music and used it as means of recreation, singing with his pupils and playing the organ for them, as he did both for himself even in his later years. Once, after he was blind, he judged a lady to be beautiful because of the beauty of her voice, which shows that he was never as old as Shakespeare's Benedick, who judged himself too old to love a woman for singing, which is to be old indeed. In his youth, Milton had declared of Leonora Baroni that her voice conveyed the sense of God's own presence.

[20] "A Musical Background for 'Lycidas,' " *HLQ*, XV (1952), 325–50. Milton speaks of Orpheus not only in "Lycidas" but in "L'Allegro," "Il Penseroso," "Ad Patrem," the Sixth Latin Elegy, and *Paradise Lost*. For Orpheus as a Christ figure in the thought of Milton's time and one of the founders of civilization, see Caroline W. Mayerson, "The Orpheus Image in 'Lycidas,' " *PMLA*, LXIV (1949), 189–207. See also Laurence Stapleton, "Milton and the New Music," *UTQ*, XXIII (1953–54), 217–26, reprinted in Arthur E. Barker, ed., *Milton: Modern Essays in Criticism* (OUP, 1965), and Nan Cooke Carpenter, "The Place of Music in 'L'Allegro' and 'Il Penseroso,' " *UTQ*, XXII (1953), 354–67.
[21] *The Merchant of Venice*, V, 1:83–88.

Either God or at least the third mind, quitting heaven, moves with secret power in your throat—moves with power, and graciously teaches mortal hearts how they can insensibly become accustomed to immortal sounds. But, if God is all things and interpenetrates all, in you alone he speaks, and in silence holds all else.

Except for Queen Christina, he never wrote with comparable extravagance of any other human being. It seems sad by way of contrast that the best he could do for his wife Betty was to tell her that she had a good voice but no ear!

On February 27, 1639, in Rome, Milton was the guest of Cardinal Barberini at the first performance of one of the earliest Italian operas, *Chi Soffre Speri*, composed by Mazzochi and Marazzuoli to a text by Rospigliosi.[22] Voltaire states, on what authority, if any, is unknown, that *Paradise Lost* was influenced by a performance of Andreini's *Adamo*, heard by Milton. All this is suitable, for, as must already have appeared, Milton's passion was largely for vocal music. He loved the blend of words and music and would probably have enjoyed the delicious, giant-scale debate as to the relative merits of the two elements which Richard Strauss achieved in *Capriccio*. So L'Allegro sings,

> And ever against eating cares
> Lap me in soft Lydian airs,
> Married to immortal verse,
> Such as the meeting soul may pierce
> In notes with many a winding bout
> Of linkèd sweetness long drawn out,
> With wanton heed and giddy cunning,
> The melting voice through mazes running,
> Untwisting all the chains that tie
> The hidden soul of harmony.

This emphasis was of course characteristic of the time, but I think it also shows something about Milton personally. For all his sensi-

[22] For the fullest study of the possible influence of Monteverdi on Milton, see John Arthos, *Milton and the Italian Cities* (BN, 1968).

tiveness to music, he was too much the moralist, too intellectual and didactic, too much interested in ideas to content himself with the beauty of sound alone; he had to have the "sense" which is poetry combined with it.

> In brief, of what use is the idle modulation of the voice if it lacks words and sense of rhythmical speech? That kind of music suits woodland singers, not Orpheus, who by his song, not his lyre, held back the rivers, gave ears to the oak trees, and by his singing drew tears from the shades of the dead. Such fame he owed to song.[23]

So Milton praised his friend Henry Lawes, whom he thought the first English composer to have matched the tone and rhythm of his music to the sense of his text, because when his songs were sung by a good singer, the text could be understood.[24]

Puritans generally have been less unfriendly to music than to dancing and theater-going, but Milton suggests no clear-cut hostility to either of these. Of course the fact that his music was primarily vocal music made it a kind of entering wedge to the theater, and the connection between music and dancing does not need to be labored. If Milton presents divine harmony in terms of music, he thinks of the creation itself in cosmic dance terms.

> We see not only the "stately Trees" rising "as in Dance" [says Helen Gardner], but the whole world coming into being as in a ballet, with the stage at first dim and empty, then gradually lightening and filling up, until at the end the whole is brilliantly lit and alive with moving figures, each performing its own graceful or vigorous part in the whole.

Much the same spirit informs Adam's recital to Raphael of his first intimacy with Eve:

> "To the nuptial bow'r
> I led her blushing like the morn; all heav'n
> And happy constellations on that hour

[23] "Ad Patrem."
[24] See Willa M. Evans, *Henry Lawes, Musician and Friend of Poets* (MLA, 1941).

Shed their selectest influence; the earth
Gave sign of gratulation, and each hill;
Joyous the birds; fresh gales and gentle airs
Whispered it to the woods, and from their wings
Flung rose, flung odors from the spicy shrub,
Disporting, till the amorous bird of night
Sung spousal, and bid haste the ev'ning star
On his hill top, to light the bridal lamp."

And at the "begetting" of the Son, the angels themselves dance in heaven.

It is not difficult to find indications that Milton *was* hostile to the theater as it existed in his day. He used classical but not apparently modern drama in his scheme of education, and he wrote *Samson Agonistes* in the classical form and even then carefully stipulated that he did not intend to have it performed. When Dryden visited him to get permission to make an opera out of *Paradise Lost*, there seems a touch of contempt in the permission he gave him to "tag," (i.e., rhyme) his verses. Yet, though he disapproved, even in youth, of the young clerics who appeared in what he considered indecent plays at the university, he never condemned drama as such nor denied having witnessed performances. In one of his 1642 pamphlets he considers the advisability of having both sports and festivals subsidized by the state, and even in the introduction to *Samson Agonistes* itself he goes out of his way to condemn those who reject theater per se and deny the existence of drama in the Bible.

What is more significant is that he originally planned *Paradise Lost* as a play, making no less than four drafts of a proposed tragedy, and this, as Dame Helen Gardner has shown convincingly, in spite of the fact that the subject is unsuited to dramatic treatment. The possible influence of Grotius, Vondel, and Andreini on *Paradise Lost* has been discussed in every edition, but fortunately we do not need to go that far afield to discern dramatic influences. Tillyard stressed the resemblances between Milton's plot and that of the morality plays, seeing Adam and Eve as the hero and heroine for whom God and the devil contend, and Hanford thinks that the guild cycles, creating a panorama of Biblical history, may have reached him through their survival as puppet shows. There can be no doubt that Milton knew his Shakespeare well, nor was he ignorant of other Elizabethan dramatists; the influence of Beaumont and Fletcher, as well as that of Plautus, upon Harapha in *Samson Agonistes* has been reasonably conjectured.

Not much can be argued from the 1630 sonnet on Shakespeare. He admires, but he is not at all specific about what he admires, and he could have been thinking about Shakespeare as a poet merely. In "L'Allegro," "sweetest Shakespeare, Fancy's child," warbles "his native wood-notes wild," but in "Il Penseroso" we turn for tragedy to the classics, while modern tragic drama of worth is dismissed as "rare." But many verbal parallels between Shakespeare and *Paradise Lost* have been pointed out and resemblances in technique and characterization besides.[25] Hanford compares Satan with Iago (in jealousy, malignity, and motive-hunting), with Richard III (in his avowal of evil), with Claudius in *Hamlet* and Marlowe's Mephistophilis in his "self-torturing remorse." Though he seems farfetched in discerning resemblances between Adam and Eve and the two Macbeths, the free use of soliloquy, the dramatic tension in the temptation scene,[26] and the

[25] See J. H. Hanford, "The Dramatic Element in *Paradise Lost*," SP, XIV (1917), 178–95, reprinted in his *John Milton, Poet Humanist*, and, for a different approach, Helen Gardner, "Milton's Satan and the Theme of Damnation in Elizabethan Tragedy," *Essays and Studies*, 1948, reprinted in A *Reading of* Paradise Lost. See also Alwin Thaler, "The Shakespearian Element in Milton," *PMLA*, XL (1925), 645–91, and George C. Taylor, "Shakespeare and Milton Again," SP, XXIII (1926), 189–99.

[26] One passage in *Paradise Lost* suggests that Milton might have made a very good film director. It occurs in Book IX, ll. 886 ff., where Eve reports her trespass to Adam,

> while horror chill
> Ran through his veins, and all his joints relaxed;
> From his slack hand the garland wreathed for Eve
> Down dropped, and all the faded roses shed.

The fading of the roses might today be called symbolism, and the last two verses sound much like a stage direction, but the effect described could not exist on the stage. Any film director who knew his business would, however, give us a close-up

33

various confrontations between Adam and Eve, especially in the quarrel scene, are undeniable, and it is in these things, rather than in specific resemblances between particular characters and situations, that the true dramatic quality of *Paradise Lost* resides.

If there was any form of dramatic entertainment that the Puritans disliked more than others it must have been the masque, which was mistrusted both for its display and its association with aristocratic extravagance and waste. It is very interesting, then, that, through "Arcades" and *Comus*, we should find Milton drawn into the masque world so early in his career. Bush finds him already a dramatic writer in *Comus*, where the great speech on the bounty of nature (ll. 706 ff.) "is a unique piece of writing; its vivid, sprawling immediacy of tactual and visual images has the effect of betraying the speaker's moral disorder,"[27] and Parker's suggestion that the fact that Milton should have permitted himself to write a masque may have displeased his father more than the mere idea of a poetical, instead of a clerical, career in itself is much more reasonable than his other idea that the poet himself could have enacted the tempter when the masque was mounted at Ludlow Castle! But there are many masque-like scenes in *Paradise Lost*, and in other poems too, even in the Nativity ode, where young Milton achieved his dedication to sacred poetry.[28]

IV

But for Milton the art of arts was, inevitably, literature, and literature, especially as he conceived it, was intimately tied up with learning. "Many a man lives a burden to the earth; but a good book is the precious life-blood of a master spirit, embalmed and treasured up on purpose to a life beyond life." Many years ago, these words were engraved around the base of the great Tif-

of the garland held in Adam's hand, and while we watched it, the flowers would fade and fall. For that matter, the movies are not the only modern form of entertainment that Milton anticipated. In Book IV of *Paradise Lost* Adam and Eve go to the animal fair, or, more accurately, it comes to them!

[27] Douglas Bush, *John Milton, A Sketch of his Life and Writings* (M, 1964), p. 111.

fany glass dome in the main room of the Chicago Public Library; later, James Branch Cabell took from them the title of his literary credo, *Beyond Life*. They constitute, perhaps, the greatest tribute that has ever been paid to books.

By the "ceaseless diligence and care" of his father, Milton was "exercised to the tongues and some sciences" from his "first years," by "sundry masters and teachers both at home and at the schools," as his age would "suffer." With at least one of the masters, Thomas Young, he established lasting and affectionate relations. What we would call his secondary education was at St. Paul's School in London, beginning, Parker thinks, in 1620 or 1621; his collegiate training was at Cambridge, beginning in 1625 when he was sixteen, which was late for the time, and which is one of a number of indications that Milton matured slowly. He seems to have been happy at St. Paul's (which was a day school), and his own scheme for the academies which he described in his tractate *Of Education* was based upon it rather than Cambridge; indeed, though he finally graduated from Cambridge with honors, and even went on to the master's degree, he never acquired much toleration for such "subtle trivialities" as were debated there (of course, in Latin), as, for example, whether or not day were to be preferred to night. Once at least he burlesqued these solemn disputations, and once he told his audience that though he did not know whether he was boring them, he was certainly boring himself. Yet debate is important in his poems all the way from "L'Allegro" and "Il Penseroso" to *Samson Agonistes*, and some scholars have conjectured that in writing them Milton was served by the training in logical disputation which he received at Cambridge. This may be true, but Milton nowhere shows any gratitude, and the tractate *Of Education* ignores university education altogether. He himself wanted to study history and science, not scholastic philosophy, he was more Platonist than Aristotelian by temperament,[29] and he had a decided bent in favor of the new humanism.

[28] See especially stanzas XI and XV.
[29] See "On the Platonic Idea as Aristotle Understood It." Hughes says that

The curriculum at St. Paul's was heavily Latinate also, and pupils were not pampered there. Hours were long, accommodations (backless benches without desks, etc.) quite impossible from the modern point of view, and discipline very strict. (If Mary Powell was distressed by her husband's beating his own pupils, this was the accepted order of the day for a schoolmaster in Milton's time.) As one of "Paul's pigeons" he would have had Latin through all eight forms,[30] Greek from the fifth, and Hebrew in his last year. The modern languages were not taught, but Milton learned French and Italian outside the curriculum.

At your expense, generous father, when I had gained command of the tongue of Romulus and the graces of Latin, and the lofty language of the eloquent Greeks, fit for the lips of Jove himself, you persuaded me to add the flowers that France boasts, and the speech the modern Italian pours from his decadent mouth, showing by his utterance the effects of the barbarian invasions, and the mysteries delivered by the Palestinian prophet.

When he went to Italy, those same decadent Italians were much impressed by the Englishman's linguistic proficiency.

For Americans, an interesting little footnote to Milton's language study relates to the year 1652, when he took lessons in Dutch from Roger Williams, then visiting in England, and discussed linguistic problems with him. But perhaps the most impressive, or even the most useful, part of Milton's education was in those areas where he taught himself. He put himself through

---

"Plato's thought is built into the ethics of Milton's poems as substantially as some parts of the Bible are built into their plots." The fullest study is Irene Samuel, *Plato and Milton* (CorUP, 1947). On Milton's use of the logic of Aristotle and/or Ramus, see Merritt Y. Hughes's edition of Milton's *Complete Poems and Major Prose* (Odyssey Press, 1957), p. 195, paragraph 46.

30 "His Latin style has not, indeed, the elegant perfection of Cicero and Virgil; it tolerates, or rather rejoices in, phrases which those writers would have deemed barbarous; but this does not come from carelessness or lack of knowledge, it is done on purpose. Milton was so much at home in Latin that he would play with it just as James Russell Lowell delighted in playing with English. It was none of your dead-and-alive schoolmaster's Latin, but a fresh and flowing diction, full of pith and pungency." John Fiske, *Essays, Historical and Literary* (M, 1902).

extensive, systematic courses of reading in the British historians, the mediaeval and modern history of Europe, theology, the Church Fathers, Renaissance and Rabbinical commentators,[31] and much besides. Nor did he suffer from the fact that it was not until long after his day that English literature became a scholastic subject. His third wife remembered how he would talk to her about Shakespeare, Spenser, Cowley, Dryden, Thomas Hobbes, and Sir Robert Howard. In Italy he remembered that he was treading in Chaucer's footsteps, and he refers to "The Squire's Tale" in "L'Allegro." Spenser was very important to him, though we have now got beyond following Greenlaw's pioneering studies in this field[32] to the extent of permitting them to obscure the basic Puritanism which, for a time, during the post-Greenlaw period, we had tended to minimize or ignore.

Science was given an important place in the academies Milton described in the *Education*—with geometry in the second year. He taught astronomy (with globes), geography (with maps), later trigonometry, but always with a practical application of what had been learned.[33] Just how much science Milton knew has always been debatable however. Basically the astronomy of *Paradise Lost* is Ptolemaic, but this may have been primarily because the Ptolemaic system supplied him with a much clearer and more manageable stage setting than the Copernican.[34] He was certainly

---

[31] The fullest studies here are Harris F. Fletcher's *Milton's Semitic Studies and Some Manifestations of Them in his Poetry* (UCP, 1926) and *Milton's Rabbinical Readings* (UIP, 1930). Denis Saurat also touches on this subject in *Milton, Man and Thinker* (DP, 1925). But it should be understood that not all scholars accept all the conclusions drawn in these books.

[32] Edwin Greenlaw, "A Better Teacher Than Aquinas," *SP*, XIV (1917), 196–217, and "Spenser's Influence on *Paradise Lost*," *SP*, XVII (1920), 320–59. Greenlaw thought Milton preferred Spenser to Aquinas because Spenser was Platonist and Aquinas Aristotelian. For a strong anti-Greenlaw statement, see Stoll, *Poets and Playwrights*, pp. 228–29, n. 9.

[33] Cf. the daring personification in "Ad Patrem": "From behind a cloud science comes forth to be viewed and, naked, bends her bright face to my kisses, unless I should find her irksome and wish to escape."

[34] Most members of my generation learned the basic facts about Milton's universe from William Vaughn Moody's charming account in his 1899 "Cambridge Edition" of Milton (Houghton Mifflin), pp. 96 ff. This has now been definitely superseded by the much more detailed and masterly account of Merritt Hughes,

not unfamiliar with the Copernican scheme, and his suggestions of incompatible vastness seem more Copernican than Ptolemaic. Marjorie Nicolson has argued for his experience of the telescope.[35] Kester Svendsen, on the other hand, shows that much of his science derived from the popular encyclopaedias of the time, thus suggesting that, in spite of all his advanced knowledge, Milton's mind was, in this aspect at least, fundamentally mediaeval.[36] If this be accepted, then we see Milton operating in the scientific field much as he did in religion, where, as we shall see, he affirmed the unquestionable authority of the Bible but interpreted it with all the freedom one might expect from the most confirmed follower of the "Inner Light."

Milton seems to have visited Galileo. He certainly knew about him, for he refers to him in *Paradise Lost*.[37] He speculated about the possibility of life in other worlds (*Paradise Lost*, VIII, 15 ff.), and I do not mean to be frivolous when I say that his marvelous description of Satan's journey in Book II is one of the most imaginative accounts we have of space travel. In Book VIII (ll. 67 ff.) Raphael describes both a geocentric and a heliocentric universe, but refuses to choose between them, which seems less unreasonable in view of the attempts of the great astronomer Tycho Brahe to work out a compromise between the Ptolemaic and the Copernican set-ups. We should always remember that the ancients had more notion of the immensity of space, and of the

---

in his *Complete Poems and Major Prose* (Odyssey Press, 1957), pp. 179–92, which includes an excellent survey of contemporary scientific problems and opinions.

[35] See her "Milton and the Telescope," *ELH*, II (1935), 1–32, reprinted in her *Science and the Imagination* (CorUP, 1956), and *The Breaking of the Circle: Studies in the Effect of the "New Science" upon Seventeenth-Century Poetry*, Revised Edition (ColUP, 1960); also Arthur O. Lovejoy, "Milton's Dialogue on Astronomy," in J. A. Mazzeo, ed., *Reason and Imagination: Studies in the History of Ideas* (ColUP, 1962).

[36] "Milton and the Encyclopaedias of Science," *SP*, XXXIX (1942), 303–27; see also his *Milton and Science* (HUP, 1956), and, for a different and much wider approach, which, however, also tends to ally Milton with the more conservative seventeenth-century trends, Richard J. Beck, "Milton and the Spirit of his Age," *English Studies*, XLII (1961), 288–300.

[37] III, 587–90; V, 261–63. See also in *Paradise Lost*, VII, 364–66, 375–78, 574–81, and compare Miss Nicolson's comment, *Reader's Guide*, 266–67.

relative physical insignificance of the earth, than they are sometimes given credit for, and that when Milton wrote about science,
he was generally riding two horses together, being both artist and
theologian.

It should also be remembered, however, that Milton was not
unaware of the dangers lurking in scientific research and especially
in the application of science to what we now call technology. Not
many years ago, the president of what is perhaps the foremost
technological school in America proved once more, if proof is
needed, that a learned man can also be a fool when he declared
that research must go on, no matter where it leads. This gentleman apparently believes that man was made for research, not research for man. (When I quoted his words in one of my classes,
a very intelligent student compared him to the physician who reported that the operation was a success but the patient died.)
Milton gives technological, like chivalric, imagery to his devils in
hell,[38] and though he presents the tree tabu in Eden as an arbitrary test of obedience, he also manages to suggest that when
Adam and Eve sinned, they broke the Great Chain of Being and,
as we should say, violated nature.

> Earth felt the wound, and Nature from her seat
> Sighing through all her works gave signs of woe,
> That all was lost.[39]

Having eaten, the hitherto innocent Eve not only proceeds to
manifest all the signs of drunkenness and nymphomania but even
proceeds to worship the tree which has become the instrument of
her ruin (a perfect example of what Dante calls following false
images of good), and at this point her idolatry is complete. The
Prometheus legend, the story of the Tower of Babel and a hundred other ancient stories and beliefs (superstitions we called

---

[38] J. B. Broadbent, "Milton's Hell," *ELH*, XXI (1954), 161–92.
[39] Milton spoils the effect of this, however, in X, 648 ff., where he has God
intervening in Creation, setting the poles of the earth askew after the Fall. If these
changes required God's fiat and intervention, then they were not inevitable results
of the Fall; instead they came into being because God wished to make the results
of the Fall even more devastating!

them, day before yesterday) all testify to man's instinctive fear of the danger to himself involved in more knowledge and power than his nature makes it safe for him to be entrusted with. Milton, like Hawthorne after him, was well aware of this, and to us who have the misfortune to live in an age shadowed by fears of nuclear destruction, his point of view can hardly seem obscurantist.

Milton's thinking was kept straight in this area by the fact that, among other things, he never forgot that the final end of learning was "knowledge of God and things invisible."

> The end then of learning is to repair the ruins of our first parents by regaining to know God aright, and out of that knowledge to love him, to imitate him, to be like him, as we may the nearest by possessing our souls of true virtue, which, being united to the heavenly grace of faith, makes up the highest perfection.

In an Edenic world, this would have been achieved in the natural course of events, but the Fall entailed intellectual as well as moral ruination, and "knowledge of God and things invisible" must therefore now require as much effort as any other kind of learning —nay, it must involve more, for being the crown of knowledge, it rests upon the foundation of all besides, which was the reason why Milton put it so late in his educational curriculum.

Moreover, it was not only in connection with science that Milton carefully differentiated between useful and useless, even harmful, knowledge. Mark Pattison long ago pointed out that he was not erudite in the sense of Usher, Selden, Voss, or Salmasius; that is, he did not value knowledge for its own sake. "His own practice had been 'industrious and select reading.' He chose to make himself a scholar rather than a learned man." He wished to know "not all, but 'what was of use to know.' " Few men with his appetite for learning can ever have been less of a mental glutton than he was, or more determined to bolt nothing but what he could digest. The poet who wanted poetry to be "simple, sensuous, and passionate" was never in any danger of becoming a metaphysical, and the scholar who stopped reading the Church Fathers when he found them tedious and trivial, with nothing to contribute to the growth of his mind, was not a pedant. In his view, as Marilla has said, "any intellectual activity that was not aimed at improving man's condition in the world was a misuse of that capacity which distinguished man from all the rest of creation—a sort of prostitution of his God-given rational faculties."[40] With him it was never a question of "What do you know?" but rather "Is it worth knowing?" and "What can you do with it?"

Milton's tractate *Of Education* has been attacked from two different points of view. The first may best be stated in the words of Richard Garnett, who saw him legislating for a "college of Miltons" and declared that his curriculum was beyond 999 out of a thousand boys and that the thousandth would die of it.[41] On the other hand, it has been objected that he was setting up a trade school.

He *was* legislating if not for a "college of Miltons," then for a selected group of young leaders, 120 in a group; from these, he hoped, the leaders of the commonwealth might spring. He was *not* thinking about universal education for the whole population, though he believed in it and elsewhere advocated state-supported schools to achieve it. Nor has he anything to say about the education of girls. In basing the curriculum upon Latin, he was less forward-looking than Comenius, but when he stressed content, not philology, and insisted that knowledge be utilized in the public service, he was in harmony with Bacon, Richard Mulcaster, and others.[42] Language interested him only as a tool, and he chose Latin and Greek and Hebrew because he thought these were the languages of those who had been most zealous for wisdom and who had most influenced our civilization. But he insisted that if

[40] E. L. Marilla, *Milton and Modern Man* (University of Alabama Press, 1968), p. 19.

[41] Garnett, *Life of John Milton* (Walter Scott, 1890).

[42] For an excellent comparison between Milton's outlook and that of Bacon, see Marilla, "Milton and Bacon: A Paradox," in *Milton and Modern Man*. No humanist—and no technologist either—was ever more concerned than Milton with man's adjustment to his environment *in this world*, but he always insists that man is basically a spiritual being, and that all his other relationships are basically conditioned by his relationship to God.

you stop with the language alone, you may well be inferior to any yeoman or tradesman who knows only his native tongue but also knows how to use it.

When we find Milton remarking incidentally that Italian may be picked up "at any odd hour," and disposing in passing of the mastery of Hebrew (and Chaldee and Syriac too), it is easy to dismiss him as an utterly impractical dreamer. But Locke said that Latin could be learned "almost in play," and Milton differed from his contemporaries less in the linguistic knowledge he required than in the use he tried to make of it. He interested his boys in natural science in terms of the world around them (in his scheme, horseback excursions over England replaced the unproductive long vacations of the universities) and gave them readings in classical authors related to what they must have observed on their fathers' estates. He also brought his pupils in contact with persons capable of giving them practical instruction in a variety of pursuits all the way from architecture to hunting and fowling, and he was far ahead of many later educators in recognizing that diet and exercise and a knowledge of medicine were as important as anything that could be learned out of books. In at least one way, American educators are much less practical and realistic than he was, for we insist upon teaching students to write before they have anything to say. Milton knew that "you can't write writing," and with him composition is the fruit of education, not the seed of it.[43]

This *is* a trade school outlook in the sense that it relates education to both public service and basic economics, but unlike what we think of as the trade school outlook today, it does not neglect either humane or spiritual values. Milton believed that teachers of Latin who use up their energies in parsing for its own sake waste far more time than language study requires, and we are

[43] For the defence of the practicality of Milton's educational schemes from the point of view of modern educators, see two articles in *Education*, one by William G. Carr, in Vol. XLVIII (1928), 618–28, and the other by H. G. Good, in Vol. XIX (1928), 40–57.

probably all familiar with modern adepts in language study who have taken a short cut through all the grammars and dictionaries and yet learned how to employ a new language with entire adequacy for their own purposes. Milton's nephews, the Phillips boys, were certainly not prodigies, but they did not die under their uncle's instruction. Milton has been ridiculed because he came home from Italy not wishing to be traveling abroad for intellectual culture while his fellow countrymen were fighting for liberty at home, yet could find nothing better to do when he got there than to open a school to instruct a few boys. But Milton thought teaching was very important, and he did not wholly give it up even when he was old and blind. Like one of the most gifted of his modern editors, he might have written,

> Heart, we have chosen the better part!
> Save sacred love and sacred art
> Nothing is good for long.[44]

Like all good teachers, Milton knew that you cannot teach anybody anything he does not wish to learn and that nothing we do for any other reason than love is any good. I am sure he was better with the bright students than he was with the dull ones, but I know no teacher of whom that is not true. We are told that he taught even arithmetic as a game, and Thomas Ellwood says that he "gave me not only all the encouragement but all the help he could." Moreover, "having a curious ear" (and—may we add?— a divining spirit), "he understood by my tone when I understood what I read and when I did not, and accordingly would stop me, examine me, and open the most difficult passages to me." And this brings us at last, I think, to Milton's own writing, where, for posterity at any rate, he made the ultimate and most distinguished use of his knowledge and of all his other resources.

[44] William Vaughn Moody, "Song-Flower and Poppy." The fact that Moody's Milton scholarship has now long been superseded should not be permitted to cause us to forget that it was considerable for its time. Judged by modern standards, he did not *know* very much about Milton, but being himself a great poet and a great spirit, he *divined* a great deal.

V

In one of the most famous tributes any great poet ever paid to another, Wordsworth wrote of Milton:

Thy soul was like a Star, and dwelt apart:
Thou hadst a voice whose sound was like the sea:
Pure as the naked heavens, majestic, free,
So didst thou travel on life's common way,
In cheerful godliness; and yet thy heart
The lowliest duties on herself did lay.

Because they so well catch the sublimity which was Milton's keynote in his *Paradise Lost* phase and pay deserved meed of praise to his idealism, these lines are often accepted at face value. Yet it would be difficult to write anything about him which should be more misleading.

His soul was like a star that dwelt apart—this man who laid aside his poetical ambitions and buried "that one talent which is death to hide" to serve as official propagandist for Cromwell's government, and who refused to relinquish this task even after he had been warned that, if he persisted, the loss of his eyesight would be required of him? Then where shall we look for the poet who did *not* dwell apart from the passions and the exigencies of his time?

There have also been those who maintained that he was somewhat worse than foolish for doing this. And certainly the tone of his controversial pamphlets supplies them with plenty of ammunition. Milton calls his opponents fool, beetle, ass, blockhead, slanderer, apostate, idiot, wretch, ignoramus, losel, mongrel, brainworm, caitiff, pork, monster, madman, liar, buffoon, pimp, parasite, viper, loggerhead, clown, vice, French vagabond, French mountebank, Burgundian slave, phlegmy clod, cloistered lubber, filthy swine, pragmatical puppy, pragmatical coxcomb, two-penny professor, raving distracted cuckoo, mercenary advocate, hairbrained blunderbuss, witless brawler, mongrel cur, conspicuous gull, rank pettifogger, most inconstant woodcock, illiterate and arrogant presumer, basest and hungriest inditer, compost of in-iquity, devotee of Priapus, foul miscreant and a base one, man of excrement, boar in the vineyard, snout in the pickle, idiot by breeding and solicitor by presumption, Brazen Ass endorsed on the backside of posterity, and huckster at law whose jabberment is the flashiest and the filthiest that ever corrupted in such an unswilled hogshead. He reproached Alexander More with the scandals of his private life and called Salmasius "the wife of a woman, a he-wolf impregnated by a she-wolf," "a second Balaam called upon by another Balak; a very talkative ass rid by a woman . . . the image of that Beast in the Revelation," and "a second Judas." It is all very well for Milton himself to tell us that vituper-ating evil is a form of praising goodness, that justice requires both, and that only a man of unquestioned integrity can undertake the task, and Douglas Bush is quite right when he reminds us that if he had needed authority for his invective, he might easily have found it in the Hebrew prophets and the Psalmist.[45] But do we not still wonder whether the services he performed were worth the loss of a pair of eyes and the danger of leaving a great literary masterpiece unwritten? "No good man," says Mark Pattison, "without impunity, addicts himself to party."

It is true, I think, that Milton was not always successful in viewing current events *sub specie aeternitatis*. Very few who take a strong interest in public affairs can; that is one reason why we travel from "crisis" to "crisis," making a good many of them more dangerous than they would otherwise be by the interpretation we put upon them. Milton would indeed have been a wiser man than he was if he had known in advance (what he finally learned through bitter disillusionment) that neither the Commonwealth experiment nor any other form of political action was going to re-generate human nature and usher in the millennium, but this is

[45] It should be noted that Milton's own integrity did not save him from re-ceiving as good (or as bad) as he gave. Thus Salmasius called him "a puppy, once my pretty little man, now blear-eyed, or rather a blindling, having never had any mental vision, he has now lost his bodily sight; a silly coxcomb, fancying himself a beauty; an unclean beast, with nothing more human about him than guttering eyelids. . . ."

the kind of thing that persons subject to the development of the messianic complex never do know in advance. And Milton's messianism was encouraged not only by his idealism but by a certain naïveté, a simplicity, an innocence (I will not call it an essential immaturity) which always clung to him despite his formidable learning.

In spite of all this, I think it can be shown that when we take up the position which Milton's critics sometimes occupy on this question, we are merely discussing generalities, and our conclusions have very little of any value for the particular case under consideration. To us John Milton was a great poet, one of the two or three greatest in English history. To him this would have seemed a very inadequate description of himself or indication of his activities. It was not that he did not desire to be a great poet; nobody ever desired it more. But with him poetry itself was part of a larger whole.

On the authority of his brother Christopher, Milton is described by Aubrey as already engaged in writing verses at eight. In his first sonnet he himself told the nightingale,

> Whether the Muse or Love call thee his mate,
> Both them I serve, and of their train am I.

In his "Vacation Exercise" of 1628 he imitates the classics, and in *The Reason of Church Government* (1642) he looked forward hopefully to leaving "something so written to aftertimes, as they should not willingly let it die." In 1637 he wrote Diodati that God had instilled a vehement enthusiasm for beauty into him if it had been instilled into anybody:

> Not with so much labour, as the fables have it, is Ceres said to have sought her daughter Proserpina as it is my habit day and night to seek for this Idea of the beautiful, as for a certain image of supreme beauty, through all the forms and faces of things (for many are the shapes of things divine) and to follow it as it leads me on by some sure traces which I seem to recognize.

You could not ask more of Poe, with his devotion to "supernal beauty" (for Poe too was a Platonist). But Milton goes on to sound much more like Keats:

You ask me what I am thinking of? So may the good Deity help me, of immortality! And what am I doing? Growing my wings and meditating flight; but as yet our Pegasus raises himself on very tender pinions. Let us be lowly wise!

He even gave the poet his place beside the doer of great deeds: "He alone deserves the appellation of great, who either achieves great things himself or teaches how they may be achieved, or who describes with suitable dignity the achievements of others." If Sir Walter Scott had been able to believe this, he might have rated his own work higher than he did. Milton agreed rather with Walter de la Mare, who wrote that a poem is a deed, and with Joseph Conrad, who called an artist "a man of action, whether he creates a personality, invents an expedient, or finds the issue of a complicated situation." Like Scott, he had the temperament of a man of action, but his beliefs made it possible for him to be more contented with his lot than Scott could ever be.

For Milton was not Poe nor Keats neither, and what others have found of patriotism and even of love he must have found of beauty —that it was "not enough." Though he said he wrote his prose with his left hand, he would certainly have published prose even if there had been no political crisis in his time, for he was always the teacher, and the Restoration itself failed to dam the flow of his pamphlets. His last days were by far his most productive, so so far as publishing was concerned (he brought out eight or nine books in six years, including an ecclesiastical pamphlet as late as 1673), and he apparently saw nothing incongruous in alternating the publication of immortal verse with what we would call schoolbooks.

There is much more prose than verse in the Columbia Edition of Milton, and though it is hard for us either to remember or to realize it, he achieved his fame through prose, not verse. It was the attack on Salmasius and its sequelae which caused his name to ring through Europe and won him the admiration of Queen

Christina of Sweden, so that continental visitors to England wanted to see first Cromwell and then him, and when he married Katherine Woodcock somebody wrote, inaccurately but revealingly, under his name in the register, "This is Milton, Oliver's secretary." As late as 1673, he received a bequest of a hundred pounds, which had been left to "Mr. John Milton, who wrote against Salmasius." From the point of view of his own time, and even if he had been willing to look at his career from a purely personal standpoint (which he never did), the consolation he gave himself after going blind, that he had lost his eyesight

> In liberty's defense, my noble task,
> Of which all Europe talks from side to side

was considerably less unreasonable than it may seem to us.

It seemed to me that, by a certain fatality in my birth, two destinies were set before me: on the one hand, blindness; on the other, duty—that I must of necessity suffer the loss of my eyes, or desert a supreme duty. . . . And so I remembered that there were many who had purchased a less good with a greater evil, glory with death, whereas I, on the contrary, proposed to purchase a greater good with a less evil, that is, at the price of blindness only, to perform one of the noblest acts of duty. Duty, being essentially more substantial even than glory, ought, therefore, to be more desired and venerated. And so I decided that the use of light, which would be allowed me so short a time, ought to be enjoyed with the greatest possible service to my countrymen.

His development as a poet, on the other hand, was slow (as Rose Macaulay says wittily, he "was not to be hurried, even by immortality"),[46] and he was reasonable enough when he complained to Diodati of his "tardy moving" and at the same time repelled the notion that he was giving himself up to studious delight for the sheer enjoyment of it and with no clearly defined goal before him. About the same time, he was complaining that his

[46] *Milton* (H, 1935).

48

"late spring" showed "no bud or blossom," and he never brought out a collection until 1645, when he was thirty-seven years old. Many of the sonnets were called forth by specific occasions, and he cannot begin "Lycidas" without apologizing for the fact that the death of Edward King has compelled him to break the resolution of poetic silence that he had taken. This, as it were, "journalistic" strain in Milton's temperament is one reason why he always gives the impression of examining controversial subjects like a committed advocate rather than an open-minded scholar. But it also means that he never created in a vacuum, as many artists do, especially modern artists, who often pride themselves upon being remote from their times or even opposed to them, and this is very important.[47] So it was that though he admits that his service for the Commonwealth took him away from what at the time would have been far more congenial pursuits, Milton could not regret it because he believed that nothing was nobler than the vindication of liberty. With him it was not a matter of being original or unoriginal, literary or journalistic. Like Browning ("Why I Am a Liberal"), he thought the poet committed to the cause of liberty through the mere fact of his being a poet. Basically the question

[47] Though he, of course, lacked the knowledge of a modern Milton specialist, Lowell (*Among My Books*) is interesting on this point: "Neither in politics, theology, nor social ethics, did Milton leave any distinguished trace on the thought of his time or in the history of opinion. In all these lines of his activity circumstances forced upon him the position of a controversialist whose aims and results are by the necessity of the case desultory and ephemeral. . . . He has no respect for usage or tradition except when they count in his favor, and sees no virtue in that power of the past over the minds and conduct of men which alone insures the continuity of national growth and is the great safeguard of order and progress." Again Lowell says: "He was far more rhetorician than thinker. The sonorous amplitude of his style was better fitted to persuade the feelings than to convince the reason." Emerson, too, declares that "Milton seldom designs a glance at the obstacles to be overcome before that which he proposes can be done. There is no attempt to conciliate, —no mediate, no preparatory course suggested,—but, peremptory and impassioned, he demands, on the instant, an ideal justice." He also complains that "he writes whilst he is heated; the piece shows all the rambles and resources of indignation, but he has never *integrated* the parts of the argument in his mind." The last objection comes oddly from a writer so notoriously indifferent to logical organization as was Emerson. Lowell himself remarked of one of the Concord poet's lectures, "It was as if, after vainly trying to get his paragraphs into sequence and order, he had at last tried the desperate expedient of *shuffling* them. It was chaos come again, but it was a chaos full of shooting-stars, a jumble of creative forces."

49

was simply whether a man was going to do his duty in his day and generation.

Milton believed the poet dependent upon inspiration to begin with, being directly indebted to "that eternal Spirit who can enrich with all utterance and knowledge, and sends out His seraphim with the hallowed fire of His altar to touch and purify the lips of whom He pleases," but he also believed that to this must be added "industrious and select reading, steady observation, insight into all seemly and generous arts and affairs," and much besides. It took him many years to acquire this, and when we realize what he acquired we can hardly wonder. Nobody would compare Longfellow's learning to Milton's (though he was one of the most learned of American poets), but Longfellow stopped writing for eleven years (aet. nineteen to thirty) because, as Robert Stafford Ward has shown, he felt that he could make no further progress "until after he had subsumed in his experience the literatures of Northern Europe as well as the Romance ones."[48] Just when Milton gave up the idea of ordination we do not know, but he not only took two degrees at Cambridge but continued his independent study and reading for nearly six years without any clearly defined goal, at least so far as anybody except himself could see. We have often assumed both that we lost the projected King Arthur epic because of Milton's Commonwealth service and that we should have lost *Paradise Lost* too if it had not been for the still somewhat puzzling clemency of the Restoration government and Milton's own almost superhuman stamina. But he might not have written *Paradise Lost* earlier than he did even if he had not written the pamphlets, for the whole course of study which produced the *Christian Doctrine* was but one of many preliminaries for it. What is more, *Paradise Lost* had to be lived for as well as read for, and even if we believe that Milton sometimes behaved unwisely in his living, may not even that have been a necessary preparation for a poem which was to present so much of both angelic and human folly? From this point of view, the pamphlets and the

48 See Edward Wagenknecht, *Henry Wadsworth Longfellow, Portrait of an American Humanist* (OUP, 1966), pp. 120–23.

whole Commonwealth experience, though generally viewed as a handicap, may have been rather a part of Milton's necessary preparation. If he was not born with the knowledge, he learned early in the game that he who would write of eternal matters in a poem which is to live through time must himself learn how to defy time in executing his task. And if God takes him (as He took Edward King) before he has been able to achieve his goal—well, then there is nothing for it but that God must accept His share of the responsibility!

With regard to King Arthur the situation was different. If conditions had not been what they became, Milton might well have given the English people a kind of national epic centering around Camelot.[49] There can be no doubt that at one time he very much wanted to do it. As he wrote to Manso:

O if my fate would grant me such a friend, who knows well how to honor the votaries of Phoebus—if ever I shall call back into verse our native kings, and Arthur waging wars even under the earth, or shall tell of the great-hearted heroes united in the invincible fellowship of the table; and—if only inspiration be with me—I shall break the Saxon battalions under British arms!

In the "Epitaphium Damonis" he seems to imply that he has actually begun work on it, and here he speaks of bringing Trojan ships to England, thus developing the connection between ancient Troy and modern Britain that the old chroniclers believed in. "And then, my pastoral pipe, if life still remains to me, you shall hang forgotten on an old pine far away; or else, changed, you shall sound forth a British theme in native strains!" But, though he continued to be interested in the subject for a long time, that is the last we hear about it in any very definite way. It has been argued that he gave it up because he came increasingly to doubt

[49] *Paradise Lost*, though something greater, is also, as Milton realized, something different; it deals not with the English people but with mankind, or at least with that portion of mankind which accepts the Christian explanation of sin and redemption. As for *Beowulf*, it exists in what, so far as the average English reader is concerned, is as much a foreign language as Latin, and until the nineteenth century it remained wholly *terra incognita*.

51

the historicity of Arthur (which would have been enough to dis-
qualify him as an epic hero for a seventeenth-century writer)—
and Milton was speaking more disrespectfully of antiquarians and
monkish chroniclers as time passed—and that he wanted not a
provincial subject but a subject of universal appeal. (The references to Arthurian matters in *Paradise Lost* and *Paradise Regained*
are beautiful, but Milton makes it clear that he regards the materials as "feigned.") These factors may well have operated, but
his increasing estrangement from mediaeval military and chivalric
ideals in favor of modern and contemporary ideals was probably
much more important.[50] At the beginning of Book IX he tells us
that he was

> Not sedulous by nature to indite
> Wars, hitherto the only argument
> Heroic deemed, chief mast'ry to dissect
> With long and tedious havoc fabled knights
> In battles feigned (the better fortitude
> Of patience and heroic martyrdom
> Unsung), or to describe races and games,
> Or tilting furniture, emblazoned shields,
> Impresses quaint, caparisons and steeds,
> Bases and tinsel trappings, gorgeous knights
> At joust and tournament; then marshaled feast
> Served up in hall with sewers and seneschals;
> The skill of artifice or office mean,
> Not that which justly gives heroic name
> To person or to poem.

We know, since he tells us, that he wanted a hero who might serve
as a pattern or model Christian, and he seems to have come in-

---

[50] For two different points of view on this matter, see Roberta F. Brinkley,
Arthurian Legend in the Seventeenth Century (JHP, 1932), especially pp. 126–41,
and George Williamson, "Milton the Anti-Romantic," *MP*, LX (1962), 13–21,
reprinted in his *Milton and Others* (UCP, 1965). Burton O. Kurth studies Milton's
epics against the background of the concept and practice of seventeenth century
Christian epic based on the Bible in *Milton and Christian Heroism* (University
of California Press, 1929).

creasingly to doubt that Arthur could serve this purpose. As for the national glory, he satisfied himself by celebrating it in the *Second Defense* and in the *History of Britain*, which has been warmly praised by Sir Charles Firth, wherein he scrutinizes the credentials of the old chroniclers as carefully as it could be done in his time, attacking Geoffrey of Monmouth and sometimes taking up an anti-British point of view.

This is obviously not the place to try to summarize Milton's sources. A whole library has been written about them, and the only advice I can give to the reader who would attain a good general knowledge of the subject is that he work carefully through the notes in the editions of Milton's poems edited by either Merritt Hughes or Douglas Bush.[51] He will finish, I think, with the conviction that Milton must have had the whole Bible and much of classical literature so close to the top of his mind at all times that he could summon ideas, characters, and phraseology at will whenever he had need of them, and he may well conclude also that his editors must come close to matching him in this regard before they can be of much use to his readers. We may take the obvious things for granted—the use of Genesis for the story of the Fall and of Luke's Gospel for Christ's temptation. But Genesis is elaborately interwoven with all the rest of the Bible and with the classics and much besides, and Job's contribution to *Paradise Regained* was secondary only to Luke's own. Most retellings of Bible stories are failures because the narrator does not know how to do anything except leave something out. Milton amplifies,[52] and the amplifications have value both for explication and because of what they themselves create. But his interweaving of themes and motifs, and the way in which one story can be used to rein-

---

[51] See also H. F. Fletcher, *The Use of the Bible in Milton's Prose* (UIP, 1929) and James H. Sims, *The Bible in Milton's Epics* (University of Florida Press, 1962).

[52] See the excellent examples cited by Nicolson, *Reader's Guide*, pp. 265–70. On a much smaller scale, Walter de la Mare did the same thing in his *Stories from the Bible*, retold for children, new edition (Knopf, 1961), making this the only book of its kind worth reading for its own sake, and not simply because the child is not yet ready to tackle the Bible at first hand.

force and dignify another—all this is more impressive than any demonstration of borrowing can be. The classics are equally well remembered and adapted; thus *Comus* comes from the Circe episode in the *Odyssey*, the vision of the future vouchsafed to Adam in *Paradise Lost*, Books XI and XII, is obviously indebted to Book VI of the *Aeneid*, and the picture of Sin sprung from the forehead of Adam can hardly have been created without remembering the birth of Pallas Athena in classical mythology. The *Areopagitica* is a model classical oration, and *Samson Agonistes* the only great classical drama ever written in English.[53]

Nor was more recent literature neglected. We cannot read the prologue to light at the beginning of Book III of *Paradise Lost* without thinking of the Dante of the "Paradiso," and we must suppose Ariosto, Tasso, and Camoëns to have had some influence upon Milton's epic plans generally. He certainly used the Italian sonnet and *canzone*. Hughes may be right in feeling that "there is more of Malory in *Paradise Regained* than appears on the surface."[54] Among English writers, Spenser and Spenser's followers, including Joshua Sylvester, with his translation of *The Divine Weeks and Works* of Du Bartas, must have been most important. But Milton must surely have remembered that if Spenser was his master, then Chaucer had been Spenser's. He surely had Spenserian allegory in mind when he referred in "Il Penseroso" to

> aught else great bards beside
> In sage and solemn tunes have sung,
> Of tourneys and of trophies hung,
> Of forests and enchantments drear,
> Where more is meant than meets the ear.

Spenser's influence upon the Sin and Death allegory is obvious, and the influence of the Sir Guyon episode in *The Faerie Queene* upon the temptation in both *Paradise Lost* and *Paradise Regained* has been elaborately argued. "L'Allegro" and "Il Penseroso," on

[53] See William Riley Parker, *Milton's Debt to Greek Tragedy* (JHP, 1937).
[54] Merritt Y. Hughes, "The Christ of *Paradise Regained* and the Renaissance Heroic Tradition," *SP*, XXXV (1938), 254–77.

the other hand, are in the Jonson tradition, and scholars have observed many echoes of Shakespearean phraseology in *Paradise Regained* and elsewhere.

But it helps to bring Milton closer to us—and it shows too the eager, prehensile quality of his mind and his capacity for embracing stimuli drawn from any quarter—that he should also have made use of materials drawn from popular superstitions and from the area that, long after his time, was to be called folklore. His folklore passages are not extensive, but some of the most beautiful in English literature are among them. Take the ghosts and fays in the Nativity ode, where the wandering dead troop home to churchyard at cockcrow, quite as in *Hamlet* and *A Midsummer Night's Dream*, and the Queen Mab and Robin Goodfellow material in "L'Allegro." Nobody has ever written anything lovelier in kind than the passage at the end of Book I of *Paradise Lost* about the

> faery elves,
> Whose midnight revels by a forest side
> Or fountain some belated peasant sees,
> Or dreams he sees, while overhead the moon
> Sits arbitress, and nearer to the earth
> Wheels her pale course;

and this seems the more remarkable because it follows so closely the wonderful description of the fall of Mulciber,

> thrown by angry Jove
> Sheer o'er the crystal battlements: from morn
> To noon he fell, from noon to dewy eve,
> A summer's day; and with the setting sun
> Dropped from the zenith like a falling star,
> On Lemnos th'Aégean isle,

which is so much more classical both in theme and in feeling. But *Paradise Lost*, like the Gothic cathedral, has such scope and range that it can accommodate passages of such opposite tenor and tone

55

as these, almost side by side, without creating any sense of violated unity.[55]

Essentially, however, Milton had not, in his own view, been born into the world to write either poetry or prose: he had been sent to serve God, and everything he wrote and everything he did must be related to that end. His talent was a trust for which he was responsible, and when the trumpet was blown, it was not for him to debate whether or not he should take the field. Perhaps the basic difficulty we have in understanding him derives from our own disposition to ignore this wonderful singleness of purpose. Yet his very simplicity involves complications of its own. He was a devout Christian who inherited the outlook of an Old Testament prophet and at the same time subsumed the culture of the Renaissance. He derived his notion of his function "from the traditions of humanism and Christianity, with the Platonic philosophy mediating between them."[56]

It had been simpler in the early days when he thought his service was going to take the form of becoming a Christian priest. Actually he did not so much abandon this idea as outgrow it. Dissatisfaction with the conditions prevailing in the English church, so sternly excoriated as early as "Lycidas," must have exercised an influence, but the basic reason surely was that the priesthood could not accommodate all there was of him. Generally speaking, the best of his early poems were not distinctively religious in their inspiration: though he succeeded gloriously with the Nativity ode, he was bound to fail with his poem on the Crucifixion. And

---

[55] Milton rejected what he regarded as superstition, but he did not lack interest in the occult, and even in *Paradise Lost* he commands the true Gothick shudder when he speaks of

> the night-hag, when called
> In secret, riding through the air she comes,
> Lured with the smell of infant blood, to dance
> With Lapland witches, while the laboring moon
> Eclipses at their charms. (II, 662–66)

See Marjorie Nicolson, "Milton and the Cabbala," *PQ*, VI (1927), 1–18; cf. E. C. Kirkland's unpublished Northwestern University dissertation, "Folklore in Milton's Major Poems."

[56] J. H. Hanford, *John Milton, Englishman* (Crown, 1949), p. 42.

may not this be the basic reason for his late development as a poet—that he had to reconcile his Hellenism with his Hebraism before the verse could become the adequate expression of the whole man? Some persons who have no religion are obliged to try to turn art itself into a religion, lest they should have no foundation whatever left for their lives. Milton made no such mistake. Though he knew that there is such a thing as secular poetry, and that it has its legitimate place, he also knew that the kind of poetry he really wanted to write could only be produced "by devout prayer to that eternal Spirit who can enrich with all utterance and knowledge, and sends out His seraphim with the hallowed fire of His altar to touch and purify the lips of whom He pleases." And he knew too that "he who would not be frustrate of his hope to write well hereafter in laudable things, ought himself to be a true poem, that is, a composition and pattern of the best and honorablest things, not presuming to sing high praises of heroic men or famous cities unless he have in himself the experience and the practice of all that which is praiseworthy."

The anonymous biographer says justly of Milton that he conceived of his talent as something "entrusted" to him. He wrote to "justify the ways of God to men," that God might be praised and man learn to live in harmony and fellowship with him. If he could hear his posterity debating whether or not *Paradise Lost* was a "true epic," he would think they were fools. Of course it is not what they understand by an epic. It was never meant to be. From the beginning Milton knew he was doing something new and different,

> Not less but more heroic than the wrath
> Of stern Achilles.

As early as *The Reason of Church Government*, he speaks of performing Homer's task for England, "with this over and above, of being a Christian." His adventurous song must "soar" with "no middle flight" above "the Aonian mount," "th'Olympian hill," and "the flight of Pegasean wing," pursuing "things unattempted yet in prose or rhyme." Even in the much quieter *Paradise Re-*

gained he is out "to tell of deeds / Above heroic." And Dryden was more perspicacious than many of his successors when he said, "This man cuts us all out, and the ancients too."[57]

Just what Milton meant by his Muse has been much discussed, but one thing is certain: he did believe that the kind of poetry he was interested in could only be achieved through God's guidance. "Milton's addresses to the Muse are too passionate to be merely imaginative flights," wrote George Edward Woodberry; "they are poetic prayers to a real presence."[58] So he remembered the Power that had inspired Moses,[59]

> That shepherd who first taught the chosen seed
> In the beginning how the heav'ns and earth
> Rose out of Chaos,

and prayed the Celestial Light to

> Shine inward, and the mind through all her powers
> Irradiate, there plant eyes, all mist from thence
> Purge and disperse, that I may see and tell
> Of things invisible to mortal sight.

There are times when Milton seems to affirm that he lived as poet in a perpetual state of inspiration. Thus, at the beginning of *Paradise Regained*:

> Thou, Spirit, who led'st this glorious Eremite
> Into the desert, his victorious field
> Against the spiritual foe, and brought'st him thence
> By proof the undoubted Son of God, inspire,
> As *thou art wont*, my prompted song, *else mute*. [Italics mine.]

[57] Northrop Frye, *Five Essays on Milton's Epics* (RKP, 1966) remarks that in Milton's time "the huge, impossible ideal, would be a poem that derived its structure from the epic tradition of Homer and Virgil and still had the quality of universal knowledge which belonged to the encyclopaedic poem and included the extra dimension of reality that was afforded by Christianity." See also Chapter I, "Milton's Theory of Poetry," in John S. Diekhoff, *Milton's* Paradise Lost, A *Commentary on the Argument* (ColUP, 1946).
[58] *Great Writers* (McClure, 1907).
[59] See J. H. Hanford, " 'That Shepherd, Who First Taught the Chosen Seed': A Note on Milton's Mosaic Inspiration," UTQ, VIII (1939), 403–19.

In *Paradise Lost* too he speaks

> Of my celestial patroness, who deigns
> Her nightly visitation unimplored,
> And dictates to me slumb'ring, or inspires
> Easy my unpremeditated verse,

which is almost mediumistic. Even in the Martin Bucer pamphlet, Milton claims to be "a passive instrument."

All this, however, implies less arrogance in Reformation times than it would today, for Reformation theologians believed that all men were inspired. Perhaps, after all, Harriet Beecher Stowe was more modest than we have given her credit for being when she said that God wrote *Uncle Tom's Cabin,* for was she not disclaiming credit she might easily have assumed to herself, and really making herself a much less important person than Lincoln made her when he humorously described her as the little lady who made this big war? The same may well be true of Milton when he writes of his work,

> if all be mine,
> Not hers who brings it nightly to my ear.

The biographer Lytton Strachey once remarked that it was almost as difficult to write a good life as to live one, and Northrop Frye draws an interesting analogy between the Christian life and the poet's way, as Milton conceived it:

> A Christian has to work hard at living a Christian life, yet the essential act of that life is the surrender of the will; a poet must work hard at his craft, yet his greatest achievements are not his, but inspired.

It must be granted, however, that the singleness Milton achieved by his failure to understand how any but a good man could be eloquent and his insistence that a bad book must be the work of a bad man had its disadvantages, and calling his opponents "snout in the pickle" was perhaps the least of them. "Defence" can be as dangerous for men as for nations. And this brings us back to Milton's power-urge and the charges which his enemies, ancient and modern, have brought against him. In other words, it brings us from Milton as Adam to the consideration of Milton and Satan.

II

MILTON AND SATAN

I

The Blake-Shelley view that Satan is the hero of *Paradise Lost*, which, very briefly and roughly, is that since Milton was a rebel he must have sympathized with the archrebel, now has no critical standing whatever. Nor will it help much to psychologize it by arguing that Satan represents the part of Milton's mind of which Milton disapproved. Milton was a human being, with the faults and weaknesses of a human being, and, since he was not a fool, he was aware of this. He knew, therefore, that, insofar as he was a sinner, he was, like all fallen men, of the devil's party. But this is not to say either that he sympathized with Satan or that he regarded these tendencies in himself as anything other than dangerous forces to be guarded against with ceaseless vigilance.

The only phase of the question that could possibly be thought of as still open in our time is whether or not C. S. Lewis went too far when, in his brilliant demolition of the Blake-Shelley view,[1] he stripped Satan of all heroic qualities and set up the counterthesis

[1] *A Preface to Paradise Lost* (OUP, 1942).

that the devil is an ass. S. Musgrove[2] thought so, seeing Lewis as too intellectual, too exclusively the theologian and moralist, not sufficiently the literary critic, or even sensitive reader, in his interpretation.

> Mr. Lewis . . . should know that the intellectual impression is only part of the total impression left by any poetical experience. Satan's initial grandeur is too great to be dismissed on the point of a non sequitur; if we are not stirred by it, against our reason and against our will, we are missing the titanic proportions of the struggle between good and evil.

This was also the view of E. E. Stoll, who insisted that, though consistently evil, Satan is also heroic.[3] But neither of these writers was ever in any danger of glorifying Satan or obscuring the lines of demarcation between right and wrong which Milton so carefully drew.

Whatever Milton might have intended as a theologian, he could hardly have created a contemptible Satan to appear as one of the leading actors in an epic poem, for this would have undercut the heroic quality of the poem itself and deprived the immortal antagonist God of due meed of credit for conquering him. But he could—and did—remember that Satan, though an archangel, was an "archangel ruined," and an archangel ruined is still an archangel, quite as, to quote Chesterton, a bad poet is still a poet and a bad man is still a man. So he could permit himself impressive use of the conventional device of epic glorification in describing both Satan and his followers, allow stylistic magnificence to the fiend himself, cause him to behave more heroically than any of his followers, and have him voice a noble expression of what William James was to call "the will to live."[4] But he could

---

[2] "Is the Devil an Ass?" RES, XXI (1945), 302–15.

[3] "Give the Devil His Due," RES, XX (1944), 108–24, and "A Postscript to 'Give the Devil His Due,'" PQ, XXVIII (1949), 167–84.

[4] Hazlitt long ago acutely observed that "the deformity of Satan is only in the depravity of his will: he has no bodily deformity to excite our loathing or disgust. . . . Milton was too magnanimous and open an antagonist to support his argument by the bye-tricks of a hump and cloven foot. . . ." Tillyard notes that "his Hell, unlike Dante's, had no human inhabitants. To make it interesting Milton

also—and again he did—show all the heroic qualities as perverted in him, and therefore more repellent than their opposites would be, since, as Shakespeare says, "lilies that fester smell far worse than weeds." Hughes calls Satan the "archetypal tyrant." He is the archetypal demagogue too, and every trick that twentieth-century demagogues have used—every logical contradiction, every confusing inconsistency—can be located somewhere in his address to his followers at the beginning of Book II and in his approach to Eve in the temptation scene. He cannot serve (for he would rather reign in hell than serve in heaven), and forgiveness is impossible for him because "disdain forbids" him to repent. Samson can find forgiveness, Adam and Eve can find forgiveness because, having sinned, they can admit their fault and reconcile their wills to that of God in striving to overcome it, but Satan never gets beyond a bitter indictment of God for having wronged him, and all his labors are dedicated to making bad conditions worse. Beginning by deceiving others, he ends by deceiving himself; by the time we reach *Paradise Regained*, he cannot comprehend the plain words of Christ even when spoken through human lips.[5] In *Paradise Lost* he has not yet got that far, so that he is truly moved by Eve's innocence and beauty, but we do not usually admire those who, like Angelo in *Measure for Measure*, are drawn toward innocence only to corrupt it. The Sin-Death allegory is a horrible parody of the Trinity, and as God became man, so Satan becomes a snake.[6] And as Dr. Jekyll at first needed drugs to release the evil in himself but finally found himself possessed by it without drugs,

was forced in compensation to humanize his devils rather than to make them represent essential evil." "A Note on Satan," *Studies in Milton* (CW, 1951).

[5] Z. S. Fink, "The Political Implications of *Paradise Regained*," *JEGP*, XL (1941), 482–88.

[6] "From hero to general, from general to politician, from politician to secret service agent, and thence to a thing that peers in at bedroom or bathroom windows, and thence to a toad, and finally to a snake—such is the progress of Satan."— C. S. Lewis. Northrop Frye argues convincingly that though Satan seems active and resourceful, he is actually "the power that moves toward the cessation of all activity, a kind of personal entropy, that transforms all energy into a heat-death." Milton believed that sin was not action but defect: "For every act is in itself good; it is only its irregularity, or deviation from the life of right, which properly speaking is evil."

so Satan and all his followers at last become snakes against their will. Walter Savage Landor became one of the wisest of Milton's commentators when he remarked that "there is neither truth nor wit . . . in saying that Satan is the hero of the piece, unless, as is usually the case in human life, he is the greatest hero who gives the widest sway to the worst passions."

Milton is very careful about handling even Satan's noble-seeming utterances so that his reader shall not be taken in by them. Take

> "The mind is its own place, and in itself
> Can make a heav'n of hell, a hell of heav'n.
> What matter where if I be still the same,
> And what I should be, all but less than he
> Whom thunder hath made greater?"[7]

This begins on a high plane, but its conclusion is surely calculated to repel sympathy, even if we do not know that seventeenth-century Christians, though finding no heresy in the idea that heaven and hell were states of mind *as well as* places, would have been shocked by the suggestion that they were *only* that. Like much that Satan says, his words are true, but in a far different sense than he intends, so that there is a depth of irony about them, the point of which is directed against himself. In Book IV he cries,

> Which way I fly is hell; myself am hell.

In a sense he *can* turn heaven into hell, for he had hell in his heart while he was still there, and until he was expelled from it, there was hell in heaven. Milton speaks of

> The hell within him, for within him hell
> He brings, and round about him, nor from hell
> One step no more than from himself can fly
> By change of place,

---

[7] For a fuller discussion of this point than can be given here, see Merritt Y. Hughes, " 'Myself Am Hell,' " *JEGP*, LIV (1956), 80–94, and A. B. Chambers, " 'The Mind Is Its Own Place': *Paradise Lost*, I, 253–55," *Renaissance News*, XVI (1963), 98–101.

and in *Paradise Regained* Christ tells Satan that he was "never more in hell than when in heaven." But it is entirely beyond his capacity to make a heaven of hell, for he can only mar God's work, not share it. And if he could turn hell into heaven, it would not please him, for he does not like heaven; he would promptly proceed to turn it into hell again. Where in all literature is there a more degraded description of worship than Mammon's

> "to celebrate his throne
> With warbled hymns, and to his Godhead sing
> Forced hallelujahs"?

What could such a spirit be expected to make of the Supreme Beatitude which is the Knowledge and Contemplation and Love of God? ("Man's chief end," says the *Westminster Catechism*, "is to glorify God and to enjoy Him forever.") It was not for nothing that Milton believed that no man could be damned by God's will but only by his own. His knowledge of evil may have been slight compared to that of some of his critics, but he had seen enough of life to be well aware that many people prefer the low road to the high road even when both lie open before them.

It is in this connection that I think the scene in hell in which Satan's followers divert themselves with athletic contests, music, poetry, and philosophical and religious speculation needs to be reconsidered. Many have been amused by these hellish pastimes and have laughed at Milton's naïveté. But it is as dangerous for us to laugh at Milton as it was for Satan himself to laugh at God. We may find that, in the final reckoning, we have been laughing at ourselves.

To begin with, these spirits are newly fallen, and it is quite in character that their pastimes and recreations should still be noble. But this is not the primary consideration. When in the third book of *Paradise Regained* Milton achieved his sweeping rejection of all merely earthly good, he was, as we shall see, too honest a man not to include among his rejections the only one that could make much appeal to himself. Similarly, in *Paradise Lost*, Book II, he perceived clearly that the appreciation of music and poetry

65

is not virtuous in itself, that it is not confined to good men or in itself sufficient to ensure salvation. All these elegances appear, for example, in the brothel scene described in Book XI, and I hope it is not frivolous to suggest that, had he put his mind to it, Milton might have developed a very good orgy scene for an historical spectacle film by D. W. Griffith or Cecil B. DeMille. Of the singing of the fallen angels he writes that

> Their song was partial, but the harmony
> (What could it less when Spirits immortal sing?)
> Suspended hell, and took with ravishment
> The thronging audience.

It was not great or sound or wholesome art—it did not satisfy its hearers—for the point of view which informed it was basically warped, but technical mastery was still there. He differentiates with equal care when he comes to philosophy and theology.

> Others apart sat on a hill retired,
> In thoughts more elevate, and reasoned high
> Of providence, foreknowledge, will, and fate,
> Fixed fate, free will, foreknowledge absolute,
> And found no end, in wand'ring mazes lost.

Of everything nobody could do anything about, in other words, everything that had no close relationship to human conduct; nothing that might interest anyone who wished to practice a religion, not just argue about it.

> Of good and evil much they argued then,
> Of happiness and final misery,
> Passion and apathy, and glory and shame,
> Vain wisdom all, and false philosophy.

It was like a "bull session" in a fraternity house, where religion is said to be the next most popular subject after sex. But I have never heard of any conversions or life-commitments to the religious life effected there.

In all three of his great poems—*Paradise Lost, Paradise Re-*

gained, and *Samson Agonistes*—Milton was in a sense plot-ridden, which is to say he was dealing not merely with traditional material but with material which was regarded as sacred and whose outline he therefore could not fundamentally change. When, at the beginning of *Paradise Lost*, he directs his Muse to "say first what cause" brought about the fall of Adam and Eve, he does not have psychological motivation in mind. He is simply going to tell us what happened: after he had been cast out of heaven, Satan laid a trap for Eve as a means of revenging himself upon God. Milton never really debates the question of God's existence—in *Paradise Lost* or even in the *Christian Doctrine*—he simply assumes it. The Bible teaches that God is, and Milton believes in the Bible as the supreme authority in religion; his sole concern therefore is to interpret it correctly and consistently. To approach him as if he were a contemporary writer, interested primarily in probing human motives and the obscure sources of conduct, is to invite the same obfuscations invoked by those critics who place psychological before dramatic considerations in interpreting Shakespeare or the Elizabethan drama in general.

One might reasonably argue, I suppose, that the greatest parts of *Paradise Lost* are those least closely indebted to the Bible. Surely there is nothing anywhere in literature which displays greater power of imagination than Book II, where Milton achieves the impossible by describing the indescribable. Book IX is another matter; here the outline adheres to the Biblical pattern, but the characterization is Milton's own, and the best of it stands beside the best of the Elizabethans. The War in Heaven, I feel, is less successful because it is only a make-believe war. We know from the beginning, even if Satan does not, that God is almighty; consequently there can be no real suspense. The basic question here is not why Satan was such a fool as to challenge God. Satan might be fool enough for anything,[8] and even today men are greater

---

[8] C. S. Lewis does not think *Paradise Lost* a comic poem, but he does see a comic element in Satan's rebellion. He finds *The Egoist* "a pendant to *Paradise Lost*, and just as Meredith cannot exclude all pathos from Sir Willoughby, so Milton cannot exclude all pathos from Satan, and does not even wish to do so."

fools in war than anywhere else, but why did God permit the destruction to continue for three days when He might have closed the issue at the beginning? Was it so that the Son might have the glory of conquering where others had failed? But He, surely, stood in no need of such attestation of his worth!

Satan could have risen from the burning lake, Milton tells us in Book I,

> but that the will
> And high permission of all-ruling Heaven
> Left him at large to his own dark designs,
> That with reiterated crimes he might
> Heap on himself damnation.

Stop to reflect that the "reiterated crimes" will be committed upon you—that is, upon human beings—and you may not find the motivation wholly adequate or sensible. (Did Job ever find it quite adequate compensation for his suffering that Satan had been convinced—that is, if he was?) God did not will that man should fall, but He knew that it would occur. Now I have no difficulty in understanding (to put it in theological language) that foreknowledge is not foreordination. The people who knew that the iniquities of the Treaty of Versailles would cause another war were not responsible for that war; many of them were foremost among those who tried to prevent it. Milton wrote *Paradise Lost* to "justify the ways of God to men," and he could achieve that end only by showing that man, not God, is responsible for the world's evil. He also believed that righteousness and evil have no real meaning unless man is free to choose between them, and this, too, we may grant, but this will not help us to understand how a being whom God had created perfectly good *could* choose the wrong path. Surely even we, who are "fallen" men and women (for the story indicates our condition equally well whether it be myth or history), know that while there are many temptations to which we are only too vulnerable, there are also others to which we could not under any circumstances yield. When the Great

68

Depression was at its height, it never occurred to anybody in this country to solve the problem which confronted us by killing and eating the unemployed, yet in a sense this would have been the perfect solution. Individuals confront the same inadmissibilities. John Milton could never, under any circumstances, have been a whoremaster, for example. And though no outside force of any kind prevents my wife from putting cyanide in my coffee or me from putting it in hers, there is not the slightest chance that either of us will do this. Would we be "freer" and more highly developed human beings if we had to exercise and develop our characters by debating this "question" with ourselves and make a fresh decision at every breakfast table?

The usual approach to solving this problem in connection with Adam and Eve is to search for evidences of predisposition to evil. Millicent Bell did that in a learned and ingenious article called "The Fallacy of the Fall in Paradise Lost,"[9] but all I can say about it is that I agree with Wayne Shumaker, who replied to her,[10] that she has not explained the paradox of a sinless couple falling but has merely pushed it farther back in time, and that this does not help at all. I must say the same of Tillyard, who sees Milton resorting "to some faking, perfectly legitimate in a poem, yet faking nevertheless," and Tillyard comes very close to Mrs. Bell when he says that both Adam and Eve are "virtually fallen before the official temptation has begun." Yet he also insists that "there is no major flaw in the poem." But what is a flawed work of art if not one which resorts to trickery to secure its effects?

The truth of the matter seems to be that if we are to have the matter formulated in terms which the logical mind can completely encompass, we must give up thinking of Adam and Eve as having been created "perfect." God could not have created man in his image without giving him volition and the power to make a moral choice; neither could man possibly be "good" without having had a chance to be "bad." Because they have never faced temptation nor made a moral choice, the characters of Adam and

[9] *PMLA,* LXVIII (1953), 863–68.
[10] *PMLA,* LXX (1955), 1185 ff., where see also Mrs. Bell's rejoinder.

Eve, when we first encounter them, are as yet unformed, with the potentiality of development in either direction. At the same time, until they have disobeyed God's commandment, they are sinless, pleasing to God, and living in harmony with his will. One might say, then, that God created man with a capacity for perfection but unable to achieve it until he had confirmed his inclination toward righteousness by making a definite decision.

Charles Lamb is said once to have remarked that man luckily sinned himself out of Eden, and many years ago, in a clever but ill-advised article, John Erskine saw Adam and Eve going out into the world at the end of the poem, to embark upon a Renaissance career. Unfortunately both writers have often been echoed by persons who had no excuse for not knowing better. Thus Émile Saillens quotes Tillyard (apparently with approval): "Milton, stranded in his own Paradise, would very soon have eaten the apple on his own responsibility and immediately justified the act in a polemical pamphlet." In much the same vein, Raleigh felt that "a short stay in Eden teaches us the sad truth that we are dependent, not only for the pleasures of our life, but even for many of the dearest pleasures of our imagination on the devices 'introduced by the necessities of sin.' " In a sense, both these statements are true, but since they assume the vantage ground of the fallen men and women we have all become, they have no relevance whatever to the Eden Milton conceived.[11]

There is nothing of what the eighteenth century called primitivism—and no savagery (noble or ignoble) either—about Milton's conception of Edenic life. Adam and Eve, though innocent, are

[11] Raleigh was even less penetrating when he remarked, as he supposed, devastatingly, that "Heaven and Hell and Eden would dissolve away like the baseless fabric of a vision, a scholar's nightmare, if once they were subjected to the free scrutiny of a child." Milton has been subjected to childish scrutiny often enough, but the results have not been very impressive. Erskine's article is "The Theme of Death in *Paradise Lost*," PMLA, XXXIII (1917), 573–82. Of the numerous replies that were made to it, perhaps the most cogent was that of Arthur O. Lovejoy, "Milton and the Paradox of the Fortunate Fall," ELH, IV (1937), 161–79, reprinted in his *Essays in the History of Ideas* (JHP, 1948). For further consideration of these matters, consult H. V. S. Ogden, "The Crisis of *Paradise Lost* Reconsidered," PQ, XXXVI (1957), 1–19, reprinted in Barker's *Milton: Modern Essays in Criticism*.

intelligent, civilized people. Unlike ourselves, they are free of shame because they have nothing to be ashamed of; they do not live in a world based upon or corrupted by fraud, violence, and exploitation. But Milton makes it perfectly clear that it was not at all his idea that if man had not fallen, he would have run about naked in Eden forever, tending flowers that did not really need his care and giving the animals names they probably never used. Neither did he think of them as "Old Age Pensioners enjoying perpetual youth." Instead, Milton saw God (and he was following Saint Augustine when he did it, as Lewis has shown), intending to create

> "out of one man a race
> Of men innumerable, there to dwell,
> Not here, till by degrees of merit raised
> They open to themselves at length the way
> Up hither, under long obedience tried,
> And earth be changed to heav'n, and heav'n to earth,
> One kingdom, joy and union without end."

Raphael's words in Book V are quite in line with this:

> "Time may come when men
> With angels may participate, and find
> No inconvenient diet, nor too light fare;
> And from these corporal nutriments perhaps
> Your bodies may at last turn all to spirit,
> Improved by tract of time, and winged ascend
> Ethereal, as we, or may at choice
> Here or in heav'nly paradises dwell."

Why, then, did he not say more about it? First, because it was no part of the problem of his poem, but, more cogently, because he did not know anything about it. Milton, too, was a fallen man; he could not possibly know how we should have developed if we had *not* fallen. When, in *Androcles and the Lion*, the Roman Captain asks Lavinia to define the nature of the God she believes enough in to die for, she replies, "When we know that, Captain, we shall be gods ourselves."

II

The basic error of the Satanists, however, has concerned not perception but attitude. Not satisfied with recognizing the Satanic element, they have insisted upon glorifying it. Certainly Milton had something of the devil in him (he was a human being), and if this had not been true, he could never have created the Archfiend as the powerful character he made him; Adam unfallen, for example, could not have imagined him. But Milton's attitude toward Satanism—and toward sin—was something quite different from what they have imagined.

The roads by which a man may travel to the devil are many—greed or passion, cruelty, idolatry, of which the most popular form is to put oneself in the place of God, and immoral or unmoral group action, under which the individual conscience abdicates and the group, which has little or no conscience, takes over. These need not all be considered in their application to Milton. As we shall see in the next chapter, he was greatly interested in women, but he was never in the slightest danger of destroying himself through sensual self-indulgence. Some of the other temptations it may, however, be worth while to examine.

Money in itself was never of great interest to Milton, for his tastes were simple, and until the last years at least he always had as much as he needed. His attitude toward it was always that of a "practical" man however, and though he does not seem to have been very good at handling it, he never professed a Saint Francis of Assisi–like indifference to it.

Milton's father was a scrivener, which means that he performed a good many services which today are performed by lawyers and also sometimes engaged in brokerage and money-lending. Though Hanford's doubts about his honesty[12] seem wholly conjectural, he accumulated sufficient means to bring up his son as a gentle-

12 *John Milton, Englishman,* p. 7.

man. His combination of business acumen and aesthetic sensitiveness suggests Browning's father, and neither Milton nor Browning ever gave a thought to the necessity of earning a living. Milton's brother Christopher entered the legal profession and, in a sense, took over his father's interests, but it seems to have been understood from the beginning that Milton was the intellectual and idealistic member of the family, and even when it was supposed that he would follow an established profession, nothing but the church seems ever to have been considered. Parker estimates that his father must have spent about three hundred pounds on his son's European tour.

The purpose of the trip into Oxfordshire which got Milton his first wife, Mary Powell, was to collect a debt owed to his father. The girl's dowry was placed at one thousand pounds; Milton never succeeded in collecting it, but neither did he ever give up his claim to it. There was litigation in the course of which his mother-in-law called him "a harsh and choleric man," but hers cannot be taken as an unprejudiced opinion.

During his years in government service Milton's salary ranged from £288 to £200. Masson estimated that he had £4,000 in investments, and Hanford placed his total income at £600 a year, which was a comparatively large sum in those days. But his nephew says he lost £2,000 by bad advice, and his house in Bread Street burned in the Great Fire of 1666. He himself is said to have claimed that he had spent "the greatest part of his estate" on apprenticing his daughters, and his capital had apparently shrunk to not more than £1,000 at the time of his death.

He is credited with generosity toward those in need and was extravagant only in the purchase of books. In 1641–42 he subscribed a very large sum, for a man of his means, toward the relief of Irish Protestants.

III

A man's attitude toward himself is closely involved with his attitude toward others, and the two may well be considered together in Milton's case. John Aubrey tells us that he "pronounced the letter R. very hard—a certain sign of satirical wit." His violence as a controversialist and the billingsgate to which, as we have seen, he often descended, conventional though it was, would seem to support this. Yet he claimed to hold no private enmity against any man, and there is considerable reason to believe this. Certainly he cherished the high estimate which the Renaissance placed upon courtesy. In *Christian Doctrine* he found it a virtue inculcated by Scripture.

All Milton's violent verbal attacks were directed against people he never saw;[13] he hated both Catholicism and the institution of kingship, but he was on pleasant terms with many individual royalists and Catholics. He helped Spenser's grandson, who had become a Catholic, to regain his confiscated Irish estates; as a matter of fact, his own brother Christopher seems to have become a Catholic without unduly straining the family tie.[14] There can be no doubt that he is telling the truth when he says that when he was in Italy he never began a conversation on the subject of religion with his Catholic hosts, but that when they brought up

---

[13] He was pretty hard on the artist Marshall, however, who engraved a ridiculous and incompetent portrait of him for the 1645 *Poems*. Instead of rejecting the picture, Milton furnished the artist, who was evidently not familiar with the language, a Greek legend to engrave under it, the sense of which is as follows:

> You, who really know my face,
> Fail to find me in this place.
> Portraiture the fool pretends;
> Laugh at the result, my friends.

This was worthy of the cleverest gallant in Restoration comedy, but the laughter is not gay, and the way in which the learned man causes his unlearned brother to appear as a fool and a gull is not free of intellectual arrogance. Masson defends Milton as having taken a "prudent precaution. For, till 1670, Marshall's botch prefixed to the *Poems* was the only published portrait of Milton—the only guide to any idea of his personal appearance for those, whether friends or foes, whether in Britain or abroad, who were not acquainted with himself."

[14] For William Spenser, see Parker, p. 501. Of course Milton also tried to help those who adhered to his own cause; cf. his fruitless efforts to bring the French reformer Jean Labadie to England (Parker, p. 525). Labadie's personal reputation was not unclouded, and it looks as though Milton closed his ears to what he had heard about him. As Masson says, "To the end, he liked all bold schismatics and sectaries, if they took a forward direction."

the subject he was frank in stating his beliefs, and we could not ask more than this of a gentleman nor less of an honest man. He permitted his sonnet to Henry Lawes to appear in a book which Lawes, a Royalist, dedicated to the captive king, and he praised John Bradshaw and Robert Overton at a time when their loyalty to Cromwell was being seriously questioned.

In sharp contrast to his manners in formal controversy, Milton was always reported "sweet and affable" in private conversation. To be sure, he was also, as Lowell observes, "the last man in the world to be slapped on the back with impunity." He knew that casual social intercourse was hostile to sustained achievement, and "to babble with another stupidly" did not interest him, but he always insisted that this did not rule out "worthy and congenial friendship." When in 1657 he was asked to recommend Peter Heimbach to the English ambassador in Holland, he declared himself unable to do so, on the ground that he had little acquaintance "with those in power, inasmuch as I keep very much to my own house, and prefer to do so." But though he believed that one kindred spirit in a thousand was the most a man could reasonably expect, he seems to have had as many intimates, both old and young, as most writers have had. Fletcher has called him the first English poet who made "a regular practice of using the sonnet to praise persons whom he completely respected and admired, both men and women." The sonnets to women, like "To a Virtuous Young Lady" (IX), defending a girl against the losels who considered her a prig, and the memorial tribute to his "Christian friend," Catharine Thomason (XIV), are of interest in this connection because they show that Milton was capable of viewing women as human beings and not, like so many men, even poets, as mere necessary foci for male desire. But the most social sonnets are XX, to Edward Lawrence, and XXI, the first of the two sonnets to Cyriack Skinner. The first, which must be quoted in its entirety, shows Milton the good companion in what is perhaps the most attractively casual guise to appear anywhere in his poems.

Lawrence, of virtuous father virtuous son,
  Now that the fields are dank and ways are mire,
  Where shall we sometimes meet, and by the fire
  Help waste a sullen day, what may be won
From the hard season gaining? Time will rub
  On smoother, till Favonius reinspire
  The frozen earth, and clothe in fresh attire
  The lily and rose, that neither sowed nor spun.
What neat repast shall feast us, light and choice,
  Of Attic taste, with wine, whence we may rise
  To hear the lute well touched, or artful voice
Warble immortal notes and Tuscan air?
  He who of those delights can judge, and spare
  to interpose them oft, is not unwise.[15]

But XXI is, in one way, even more significant:

Today deep thoughts resolve with me to drench
  In mirth that after no repenting draws;
  Let Euclid rest and Archimedes pause,
  And what the Swede intends, and what the French.
To measure life learn thou betimes, and know
  Toward solid good what leads the nearest way;
  For other things mild Heav'n a time ordains,
And disapproves that care, though wise in show,
  That with superfluous burden loads the day,
  And when God sends a cheerful hour, refrains.

By 1655 Milton had learned that a man cannot always live at high tension if he would survive. There had been a time when he did not know that.

[15] "And spare/To interpose them oft" has inspired some scratching of critical craniums, having been interpreted to mean: (a) refrain from interposing, and (b) spare time to interpose. Surely Fraser Nieman, *PMLA*, LXIV (1949), 480–83, is right when he settles for the latter interpretation. As he says, Milton cannot possibly have meant to say, "Come to a frugal meal, but be careful not to come to frugal meals often"! He is supported by Elizabeth Jackson (pp. 328–29), who stresses the connection between "judge *and* spare," places the emphasis (where it belongs) on music, not wine, and points out additional Horatian echoes.

Milton did not make a god of nature, and he knew that we bring impurity with us into the world, but he consistently rejected all tendencies to hold man guilty until he is proved innocent and opposed all those who would use man's sinfulness as an excuse to rivet either political or ecclesiastical tyranny upon him.[16] He was touched by man's frailty as well as by his high potentialities.[17] Whether or not E. H. Visiak is right when he says that Milton loved men through God, not God through men,[18] he did believe that man has God's breath in his body, "part of Himself, immortal, indestructible, free from death and all hurt." "Nothing,"

[16] One of the meanest tricks I have played on my Milton students has been to ask them whether there was anything in the *Areopagitica* to prevent books from being "banned in Boston," and a good many have fallen into the trap by replying that if Milton's precepts were followed, no book could ever be banned in Boston or anywhere else. The truth, of course, is that the *Areopagitica* argues only against precensorship, which exists, officially, nowhere in the United States; the published book may still be condemned and burned by the common hangman. In other words, you are free to say anything you like, but you can still be held to account for what you have said. In an age when the pornographers have captured the theater and a good share of the publishing business, it may be well to add that Milton is protecting not obscenity but the free discussion of ideas. He disposes of those who would run open sewers through the city in a single verse: "License they mean when they cry liberty." It is interesting that he should have refused to grant the right of free speech to Roman Catholic controversialists on precisely the same grounds as those on which the late Senator Joseph McCarthy refused to tolerate Communists. (Communism, said McCarthy, is not a philosophy but a conspiracy.) Even Bernard Shaw once pointed out that nobody really believes in absolute freedom of speech. It is always a question of less or more, and adjustments and readjustments are forever being made along a very fine and shifting line. Nevertheless the atmosphere of the *Areopagitica* is considerably more liberal than are its actual provisions: "methinks I see in my mind a noble and puissant nation"; "a man may be a heretic in the truth"; etc. Milton urged upon Cromwell the repeal of all laws restricting the actions of people in their private lives, even when such restrictions seemed to be in the interest of morality, and Masson was quite right when he said of the *Areopagitica* that it breathed the full principle of toleration rather than the exceptions.

[17] Dame Helen Gardner finds that "the pilot in his small skiff," anchoring beside the whale in *Paradise Lost*, "hoping he has found safety and longing for the light which seems as if it will never come, has the frailty and the pathos with which Milton so constantly invests the human figures that he introduces through his similes into his poem." These similes "draw on ordinary life and the natural world we all inhabit. They bring before us not merely monsters of legends and heroes of antiquity, but a pilot off his course at night, a ploughman anxious for the harvest, a drunken peasant intruding on fairy revels, a burglar, a young man out for an early morning walk in the fields around a city who catches sight of a pretty girl."

[18] *Milton Agonistes: A Metaphysical Criticism* (A. M. Philpot, Ltd., n.d.)

77

he says, "is nowadays more degenerately forgotten than the true dignity of man." Moreover, he believed not only in man's dignity but also in his right to happiness. He even opposed oppressive marriage laws because it seemed to him an outrage upon human nature that people should be forced to cohabit against their will, and for all the vigor and even violence with which he attacked the subject, we sense his tenderness when he tells us how he desired "with one gentle stroking to wipe away ten thousand tears out of the life of men."

Most of this, of course, was very good Puritanism. In a way— which is hardly the modern way—it was even good democracy. You cannot conceive of man as able to govern himself and to apprehend God's truth without also seeing him as a creature of worth and dignity. You cannot rob him of the intermediary of church and priest, causing every individual to confront God directly, and making him responsible for his own salvation, without believing that he possesses a backbone equal to the strain that must rest upon it.[19] But not all Puritans had the sound metaphysical basis for belief which Milton possessed, and for the Calvinists, who believed in foreordination and election, the whole show was reduced to a species of shadowboxing, for one's ultimate fate depended upon God's arbitrary fiat and could not be affected by anything the sinner might do or fail to do.

The best testimony to Milton's human sympathy and dignity appears in his treatment of sinners in his own works. He did not create a Samson free of faults, but he did liberate him from all the loutish, clownish aspects of his personality as he appears in the Bible, where he is very much what the Elizabethans would have called a "roaring boy." But Adam and Eve are surely better examples, and they come much closer to us. If we lack the experien-

[19] Many mental backbones cracked under the strain, and Oliver Wendell Holmes was quite right when he remarked that if the poet Cowper had had a sensible priest to confess to, he would not have gone crazy over believing that he had committed the unpardonable sin. Close parallels can be drawn here between the political and the ecclesiastical sphere. Cf. in Shakespeare's *Henry V* (Act V, Scene 1) the remarkably suggestive discussion of the respective responsibility of the king and his subjects for deeds committed in warfare, whether, when the cause is not just, the soldier is responsible only to the king or also to God, etc.

tial background necessary to sympathize with them perfectly in their prelapsarian state, we do sympathize and shudder when they sin, and the pity we feel for them in their repentance is changed to admiration when they gird up their loins to go out from Eden to face all the perils and agonies of the world that we ourselves know only too well. "It is to Milton's credit," says B. Rajan, "that he finds a human problem where others see only a theological formula."[20]

IV

Milton's background and rearing was not of a sort which, a priori, would seem calculated to cause him to think meanly of himself. When he was ten years old, his father had his portrait painted which, as Parker notes, "tells us something about his tastes, something about his prosperity . . . . but even more about his growing pride in his son." There can be no question that Milton had a kind and indulgent father. If he was never called upon to condone bad behavior on the part of his son, Milton's failure to follow up on his original plans for ordination and the extremely leisurely way he went about choosing his lifework must still have created what in many households would have been a very difficult situation. "Ad Patrem" shows clearly that at one time the father had rather less sympathy with the son's poetic aspirations than the latter could have desired, but there is no indication that he was unreasonable in any way. Milton stated his position— and his aims and intentions—with force and dignity, and there does not seem ever to have been any reasonable doubt that the final decision would be his to make. We know nothing about the mother (actually we do not know very much) to indicate that she was anything but a compendium of all motherly and womanly virtues. She seems to have done her son the disservice of passing her weak eyes on to him (which he in turn transmitted to his daughter Deborah, though neither of the women went blind), but this was not her fault. Parker conjectures that Milton may

[20] *Paradise Lost and the Seventeenth Century Reader* (CW, 1947).

have been over-attached to his mother, and that his moral fastidiousness may have been affected by this, reminding us that he was twenty-eight when his mother died and still unmarried.

Though Milton was certainly not incapable, especially during his early years, of self-doubt, he frankly admits "a certain niceness of nature, haughtiness, and self-esteem either of what I was or what I might be." He was more concerned about whether the degenerate age during which he wrote it was capable of understanding *Paradise Lost* than whether he was capable of producing it, and though his refusal to let anybody tell him that *Paradise Regained* was inferior may have been due to a sincere preference for the more austere style he had then begun to cultivate, it was not uncharacteristic. He published his own letters and rated himself precious as both a blind man and a poet. He tells us that there has never been anything reprehensible in his conduct and that he never wrote anything which failed to accord with truth, justice, and piety. All in all, he would not exchange his consciousness of rectitude with that of any other human being.

That he was not ignorant of the spiritual dangers involved in pride his portrait of Satan abundantly shows. But he distinguished between Satan's kind of pride and that based on an honest self-respect. He thought about all the problems involved and tried to resolve them. A Christian, he thought, should abstain from self-commendation except when it was necessitated by the occasion. But when the cause of Christ needed to be defended, then he not only might but must speak, even, if necessary, in rough accents, and "send home his haughtiness well bespurted with his own holy water." Nor must he leave upon his own garment "the least spot or blemish" so long as God gave him the opportunity "to say that which might wipe it off." He found such opportunities often, he sometimes defended himself against insignificant persons whom it would have been more dignified, perhaps even more crushing, to ignore, and if his opponents set him the example of making his own personality an issue, he did the same with theirs. I have elsewhere collected some of the pejorative terms he employs, and he frankly admits that he enjoyed this "sport."

Calling people "snout in the pickle" was bad enough (not so much because Milton's opponents did not deserve it as because it was unworthy of Milton himself), but his attack upon King Charles I was even worse. He may well have believed that the king's grandfather had been David Rizzio rather than Darnley, for, absurd as the notion is, many have believed it since, but for a poet to make it a means of reproach against the king that, during his imprisonment, he had used a prayer from

The vain, amatorious poem of Sir Philip Sidney's *Arcadia*, a book in that kind full of worth and wit, but among religious thoughts and duties not to be named, nor to be read at any time without good caution, much less in time of trouble and affliction to be a Christian's prayerbook

—this, surely, was to display a fanaticism never surpassed by Exeter Hall.[21]

I have already said that Milton is the kind of artist who creates by dramatizing his own personality, not the impersonal Shakespearean kind, who, as Coleridge says, "darts himself forth, and passes into all the forms of human character and passion, the one Proteus of the fire and flood." I think Dame Helen Gardner goes too far when she calls *Paradise Lost* "wholly undramatic, because the dramatist himself defies the first rule of dramatic presentation by being himself present throughout, an actor in his own play," but she is surely right when she adds that he is present not only in the prologues, "in which, going beyond all epic precedent, Milton takes the reader into the sanctuary of his own hopes and fears and sorrows," and that he engages us throughout "in a story that expresses the poet's personal feelings and personal views." How much of Milton's own personality we read into *Samson Agonistes* will no doubt be determined partly by whether, with most Milton scholars, we believe that work to have been written after *Paradise Regained*, or, with Parker, assign it to a much earlier date. The subject need not be debated here, where it is perhaps enough to

21 It has been unconvincingly argued that Milton made up this charge. See Parker, pp. 964–65, n. 43.

say that though, publishing *Samson* when he did, Milton could not possibly have been unaware that, like his hero, he was the champion of a defeated cause, he could not, on the one hand, have wished to suggest that Samson's faults were his faults, while, on the other, he must have known that there were many passages in the play which his readers would not be able to examine without having his image before their mental eyes.

Nevertheless, Milton's autobiographical tendency has often been exaggerated by his critics. A creative writer may start with himself or he may start with another, but in neither case is he obliged to end where he has begun. Look, for example, at Christ's words in *Paradise Regained*:

> "When I was yet a child, no childish play
> To me was pleasing; all my mind was set
> Serious to learn and know, and thence to do
> What might be public good; myself I thought
> Born to that end, born to promote all truth,
> All righteous things."

Of course we cannot read this without remembering what kind of a child we suppose John Milton to have been. But if we are to follow the rule that it is not necessary to postulate the author's personal interest unless there is something in the passage involved not necessitated by the situation being described, then we need not take our attention from Christ at this point to focus it upon John Milton. For this is just what we should expect of the twelve-year-old who went up to Jerusalem and was found by his parents in the Temple conversing with the learned doctors upon spiritual matters, as Saint Luke records. And to make the connection inescapable Milton has Christ refer to this incident immediately after having uttered the lines quoted.

Many years ago, Sir Walter Raleigh pointed out as eminently characteristic of Milton the interesting fact that, even in the divorce controversy, he did not argue that he should be permitted to take an exception to the law; he argued instead that the law itself was wrong and must be changed. To be sure, Sir Walter also believed that Milton "learned little or nothing from the political events of his time. He was throughout consistent with himself," and Sir Leslie Stephen said that he could not "abstract his cause from himself."[22] Sir Herbert Grierson was somewhat more precise:

> No one was ever, in one way, more susceptible to experience than Milton. . . . For an experience to affect Milton it had to be *personal*. . . . No one, except perhaps Shelley, was more impenetrable by what one may call the general teaching of experience.[23]

And this suggests the principal limitation upon Milton's egoism; as Charles Williams has said, he had no use for "the self-closed 'independent' spirit." Personal experience he must have, but personal experience he used as a door through which he entered upon universal experience; this tendency, too, points up the classical element in his art. It was not for nothing that Tillyard marveled that a man with his temperament and his exalted estimate of himself and the lofty plans he had made for his life should have been able to survive the disaster of his marriage and the wreck of his political hopes. "The extraordinary thing about Milton was that somewhere in him there was a humility that coexisted with this overweeningness and which saved him when disaster came."

But not even Tillyard was always as clearsighted as this. His interpretation of "Lycidas" achieves such an unwarranted shift of emphasis as to leave him open to Logan Pearsall Smith's witty, but not, I think, unfair statement of having seen hydrophobia as the inspiration for his poem.[24] Parker, much less elaborately, though no less absurdly, has Milton worrying about his own possible death when he furnishes an epitaph for the Marchioness of Winchester, and Hanford makes him the shepherd lad in *Comus*.[25] We have always recognized that there was no close bond between Milton and Edward King, whose death furnished the occasion for "Lycidas"; this was no Alfred Tennyson–Arthur

22 *Studies of a Biographer*, Vol. IV (Putnam, 1907).
23 "John Milton," *Criterion*, VIII (1928), 7–26, 240–57.
24 *Milton and His Critics*, p. 44.
25 Parker, *Milton*, p. 95; Hanford, *John Milton, Englishman*, p. 65.

Henry Hallam situation nor anything approximating it. But Tillyard was not satisfied to stop here. If Milton was not concerned with Edward King *qua* Edward King, he argues, then he must have been thinking of John Milton *qua* John Milton.

Milton was a poet, King had written verse too. King had made a voyage on the sea, Milton was about to make voyages. How could Milton have missed the idea that *he* might make the analogy complete by getting drowned, like King, also?[26]

There is an either-or antithesis here which it is not at all necessary for the student of the poetic imagination to accept. If Milton was not greatly interested in Edward King *qua* Edward King, he *was* interested in him as a type of unfulfillment. (As Virginia Woolf might have put it, he was interested not in Edward King but in Edward Kingness.) Here was a richly endowed young man who had dedicated all his gifts to the service of his country and his God. What kind of a world is it in which such a life can be snuffed out, cast aside, wasted before (through no fault of its own) noble service has been rendered? How can a young man feel at home in such a world? How can he go on living without first having made some attempt to think this problem through?

In a sense, then, Milton *is* thinking of himself, but he is thinking of himself as a human being. Like King, like all the other men and women who live upon this earth, he is expendable. If this were not so, he might still pity King, but he would pity like an angel, not, as he does, like a man. Once again, he begins with the specific and rises to general considerations. "Ay, madam, it is common," said Hamlet to the Queen, when she tried to comfort him by reminding him that the death of fathers was quite in the way of nature. But if this sorrow had come to him alone, he might be able to endure it; it is the thought that it is a part of universal

---

[26] Tillyard, *Milton*, p. 81. *Comus* has been mauled out of all recognition, notably by the "New Critics," who could not have treated it differently if they had set out to burlesque their own methods. In "Reading *Comus*," MP, LI (1953), 18–32, reprinted in his *Ikon: John Milton and the Modern Critics* (CorUP, 1955), Robert Martin Adams brilliantly demolishes all this nonsense, displaying in the process a controversial gusto not unworthy of Milton himself.

experience that makes it unendurable. Even Tennyson felt this about Hallam:

> That loss is common would not make
> My own less bitter, rather more:
> Too common! Never morning wore
> To evening but some heart did break.

And Albert Schweitzer used to tell his African patients that a man who had been

> delivered from pain must not think he is now free again, and at liberty to take up life just as it was before, entirely forgetful of the past. He is now a "man whose eyes are open" with regard to pain and anguish, and he must help to overcome those two enemies (so far as human power can control them) and to bring to others the deliverance which he has himself enjoyed.

There is no question of egotism or self-centeredness here. On the contrary, this is the only way the human imagination can work in our present stage of development.[27]

In a man of action, self-will takes the form of a desire to dominate other men; what a great writer desires is to rule their minds. In the last analysis, however, this is the only kind of power that endures ("Rome fell, but when did Virgil fall?"), and the poet may be as avid for fame as the conqueror. In "Lycidas" Milton calls the desire for fame "that last infirmity of noble mind"—an infirmity because an ideal Christian lives only to serve God and is indifferent to reward, performing great or good deeds because they are good or great and not because he hopes to become celebrated on account of them, but an infirmity of noble rather than ignoble mind because it is impossible for the boorish, sensual man, who is not sufficiently developed as a spiritual being to be able to sacrifice present, immediate physical reward or satisfaction in the hope of winning a hypothetical, immaterial reward in the future.

There has probably been no period in the history of Western

---

[27] For a fuller discussion of this matter, see the author's "Milton in 'Lycidas,' " CE, VII (1946), 393–97.

culture when men were more avid for fame than they were during the Renaissance, and it is clear that in this respect Milton was a man of his time. Even in youth he did not wish to be lost in the crowd; if he could not do great deeds, he would celebrate them. He meditated immortality and dreamed of creating something of such worth that the world would not willingly let it die. When he compares his exile from Cambridge to that of Ovid, finds his fame insured by depositing his books in the Oxford library, or promises immortality to the army captain who shall spare his dwelling, he is being playful of course. But it is not the playfulness of a man who thinks meanly of himself.

Professor Hanford distinguishes three stages in Milton's attitude toward fame: (1) he desires it, (2) he expects opposition, (3) he looks forward to "fit audience though few." It is interestingly paradoxical that he should have disclaimed the desire in the *Second Defence*, which brought it and blindness with it, in which calamity he supported himself by the thought that he had lost his sight

> In liberty's defense, my noble task,
> Of which all Europe talks from side to side.

Even more striking, and considerably more touching, is the Prologue to Book III of *Paradise Lost*, in which, finding himself "equaled" in fate with

> Blind Thamyris and blind Maeonides,
> And Tiresias and Phineus prophets old,

he only wished he were "equaled" with them also "in renown."

In *Paradise Regained*, which disdains worldly ambition, along with every other purely earthly good, Christ knows that the "miscellaneous rabble" we call in modern times "the general public" is but "a herd confused,"

> "who extol
> Things vulgar, and well weighed, scarce worth the praise.
> They praise and they admire they know not what,
> And know not whom, but one leads to the other."

Christ's standard is altogether different.

"This is true glory and renown, when God
Looking on the earth, with approbation marks
The just man, and divulges him through heaven
To all his angels, who with true applause
Recount his praises."

Christ could live on those dizzy heights, but could Milton, who
was only a man, do the same? At least this is not a radically new
note in his poetry, for he had said practically the same thing in
"Lycidas" itself:

"Fame is no plant that grows on mortal soil,
Nor in the glistering foil
Set off to th' world, nor in broad rumor lies,
But lives and spreads aloft by those pure eyes
And perfect witness of all-judging Jove;
As he pronounces lastly on each deed,
Of so much fame in heav'n expect thy meed."

v

One subject remains. I have so far given no consideration to
Milton's share in the corporate evil of society. Mark Twain once
described the devil as spiritual head of four-fifths of the human
race and political head of the whole of it. How much application
does this have to Milton's involvement in the political revolution
of his time?

His attitude toward England and the English government
shifted notably in the course of his life. His passionate glorification
of his country in "In Quintum Novembris," which deals with the
Gunpowder Plot, may be discounted on the ground of his extreme
youth. He praises "this great and warlike nation" and identifies its
honor with his own, and in 1642 he thought being known there
was enough, though nobody could have been more elated than he
was when his pamphlets gave him a European reputation. There
are fervent passages in which the English are glorified, in round

Biblical terms, as the chosen people, enjoying the special favor of God, and he sounds like an American with a messianic complex when he beholds the nations "recovering the liberty which they so long had lost" and "the people of this island . . . disseminating the blessings of civilization and freedom among cities, kingdoms, and nations." But when the English disappoint him, in the past or in the present, he can rebuke them like a prophet, and he had only contempt for an historian who could put patriotism ahead of truth.

He gladly confessed his own indebtedness to classical culture, and he had more feeling for Italy, "the home of human studies and of all civilized teachings," than for France. When he was abroad, he tried to represent England worthily, and he does not seem to have loved her less for what he saw of other nations. What is most admirable about him in this connection, however, is his sense of brotherhood with all good men, whether Englishmen or continentals. "I do not regard any good man as a foreigner or a stranger." And again: "He . . . that keeps peace with me, near or remote, of whatsoever nation, is to me as far as all civil and human offices an Englishman and a neighbor." In a post-Restoration letter he uses words which many an exile from Nazi Germany might have echoed: "One's country is wherever it is well with one." And as early as 1638 he wrote Benedetto Bonmattei words which must today remind Americans of President Kennedy's inaugural address:

> All this I say, not because I suppose you to be ignorant of any of it, but because I persuade myself that you are much more intent on the consideration of what you yourself can do for your country than of what your country will, by the best right, owe to you.

Milton was not a political theorist: strong as they were, the recommendations to which he committed himself during the Commonwealth period were as pragmatic as anything an Emerson might have offered. He had always placed learning and righteousness far ahead of political power and seen those possessing them as enjoying "a kingdom within which is far more glorious than any earthly dominion." Hanford seems to me to overstate the case when he calls Milton "a Republican by conviction long before the outbreak of the civil war." His early writings about the Gunpowder Plot and the death of King James I reveal something more than Christian good will toward that monarch; the pamphlet *Of Reformation* (1641) makes it a virtue of the Presbyterian system that it is compatible with monarchy; as late as the *Second Defence* he insists that he is not against kings but only against tyrants, and his praise of Queen Christina of Sweden, who had sided with him against Salmasius (or so he believed) is fulsome in the extreme. As for King Charles I, Milton himself says of the *Eikonoklastes* that he undertook it as a work assigned, rather than upon his own volition, not relishing the idea of descanting "on the misfortunes of a person fallen from so high a dignity, who hath also paid his final debt both to nature and his faults." Though he was always inclined to be very personal in controversy, he had tried at first to keep the king's personality out of the discussion, and it is probably fair to say that he did not make this an issue until after the issue had been raised by His Majesty's defenders.

The Tenure of Kings and Magistrates rests ultimately upon the contract theory of government ("the power of kings and magistrates is nothing else but what is only derivative, transferred, and committed to them in trust from the people to the common good of them all"), from which it must follow that a king who abused his powers was "a common pest and destroyer of mankind." In the interest of the common welfare, it might often be advisable on pragmatic grounds to obey even a tyrant in indifferent matters, but when a real issue arose, the same consideration might decree his deposition and even his death. And Milton argues that when the government killed Charles I, they did not kill a king, for he had ceased to be a king when the power which had been invested in him by the people was recalled, which reduces the whole controversy to a conundrum: "When is a king not a king?" to which the answer must be: "When he has been deposed."

For all that, the voice of the people was never the voice of God to Milton: the Bible, the classical moralists, and his own experience had all combined to teach him that whether the explanation lay in the Fall or in some other hypothesis, very few men, in the present stage of human development, were actually capable of governing either others or themselves. "None can love freedom heartily but good men; the rest love not freedom, but license, which never hath more scope or more indulgence than under tyrants." When he wrote his *Ready and Easy Way* he was not ready to sanction the return of the king even if it should be called for by a majority vote. But he did not believe that a man can escape servitude by merely changing masters either, not even if he changes from Charles R to Oliver P. Ultimately, Milton accepted the Cromwellian dictatorship, though not without qualms, for it was axiomatic "that the most worthy should possess the sovereign power" and that "you are such, Cromwell, . . . is acknowledged by all." Milton knew that great men have sometimes saved their countries by disobeying the laws thereof; had he not defended the right of the army or the Rump Parliament to commit regicide, on the ground that it was lawful "for any who have the power" to call a tyrant to account? After Cromwell was gone, he even turned, for a moment, to General Monk, as a refuge against the impending Charles II.

In Cromwell's government, Milton's primary concern was with foreign correspondence, which was entrusted to him because of his linguistic capacities, but there was less of this than had been expected, and many other chores were entrusted to him. Though he attended some of the sessions of the Council of State, the anonymous biographer says he was "a stranger to their inner councils." Diekhoff has conjectured, upon somewhat inconclusive evidence, that, "except for his literary services," Milton was "not a very efficient secretary" and that he was "too wasteful of his energies to be a really capable man of affairs." He had "views," and sometimes he expressed them, in verse as well as in prose, and since he was himself, no doubt he also sometimes expressed them orally. After his Latin pamphlets had made him famous on the Continent, visitors to England wanted most to see him after Cromwell. But when, in 1659, Henry Oldenburg suggested his writing "the history of our political troubles," he replied that they were "worthier of silence than of commemoration. What is needed is not one to compile a history of our troubles, but one who can happily end the troubles themselves. . . ."[28]

Perhaps Milton's true position under the Commonwealth was better understood in Restoration times than posterity has understood it, and this may help to explain the somewhat puzzling fact that he escaped serious punishment, more than the other hypotheses that have been suggested from time to time—that Davenant or Marvel or Clarendon protected him, or that Charles II, who had interesting streaks of sensitivity running alongside his callousness, did not wish to take vengeance upon a blind man. Yet nothing could wholly cancel out the fact that, despite his political unimportance, Milton had achieved the most intellectually respectable defence of the regicide that had appeared. In June, 1660, Parliament ordered his arrest. His publications were burned, and he went into hiding for the summer. It is said that he feared assassination as well as apprehension. Many must have been surprised when he was not among those excluded from the Act of Pardon issued on August 29; perhaps it was crossed wires somewhere that caused him to be arrested nevertheless and held until the middle of December. The record is a puzzling, contradictory one, and however it all came about we must remember to the credit of both King Charles II and the House of Commons that they could have deprived us of *Paradise Lost* had they been so minded.[29]

The most effective means through which the state serves Satan is war, and Milton's position on war is curiously ambivalent: he furnishes pacifists about as much ammunition as any great English writer, yet he stops short of their position. When the civil war

[28] See Barbara Kiefer Lewalski, "Milton: Political Beliefs and Polemical Methods, 1659–60," *PMLA*, LXXIV (1959), 191–202.

[29] See Parker's detailed discussion, *Milton*, pp. 568–76, 1087, n. 36.

came, he had to make up his mind whether or not to serve as a soldier. He decided against it,[30] and in the *Second Defence* he tells us why: "it was only that I might earnestly toil for my fellow citizens in another way, with much greater utility, and with no less peril."

As a servant of the state, he was obliged to defend Cromwell's policies, which were far from pacifistic, though it is true that he allowed many of his deeds to go uncelebrated. He was not enthusiastic about the war with the Dutch, but he would apparently have welcomed war with Turkey, to free the Greeks, and he called the war in Ireland "most agreeable to God"! He opposed Cromwell's projected league of Protestant powers against Rome, however, believing that God would take care of Rome in his own way and his own good time, and though he had no admiration for the Rump Parliament he was shocked when the army dissolved it and usurped its power.

As a sonneteer, Milton told Cromwell that

> peace hath her victories
> No less renowned than war,

and asked General Fairfax

> For what can war, but endless war still breed?

In the *Second Defence*, war is no ultimate achiever of desirable ends, and "real and substantial liberty" must be "sought for not from without, but within, . . . principally not by fighting, but by the just regulation and by the proper conduct of life." And he adds, for the benefit of Queen Christina, that "the arts of peace surpass the stratagems of war."

The most cogent pacifist feeling must, however, be sought in *Paradise Lost* and especially in *Paradise Regained*, which is cer-

---

[30] Hanford rejects the view that Milton ever saw either military service or military training: see "Milton and the Art of War," *SP*, XVIII (1921), 232–66, reprinted in his *John Milton, Poet and Humanist*, though he is not so sure that his predecessors were right in dismissing the report that Milton was once considered for an adjutant-generalship in Sir William Waller's army; see also Parker, p. 895, n. 114.

tainly one of the great pacifist books of all time. These words from Book II of *Paradise Lost* represent perhaps the most extended passage of direct moralizing in all Milton's poetry:

> Devil with devil damned
> Firm concord holds, men only disagree
> Of creatures rational, though under hope
> Of heavenly grace; and God proclaiming peace,
> Yet live in hatred, enmity, and strife
> Among themselves, and levy cruel wars,
> Wasting the earth, each other to destroy:
> As if (which might induce us to accord)
> Man had not hellish foes enow besides,
> That day and night for his destruction wait.

But if this is the most direct passage, it is not the most important. For we cannot understand anything about *Paradise Lost* if we do not remember that Milton proposed to begin where other epic poets left off. As we have seen, he was

> Not sedulous by nature to indite
> Wars, hitherto the only argument
> Heroic deemed,

nor did the "long and tedious havoc" of "fabled knights / In battles feigned" attract him,

> races and games,
> Or tilting furniture, emblazoned shields,
> Impresses quaint, caparisons and steeds,
> Bases and tinsel trappings, gorgeous knights
> At joust and tournament.

That kind of thing he had left behind him with the fading of Arthur from his epic plans. What interested him now was

> the better fortitude
> Of patience and heroic martyrdom
> Unsung.

93

In *Paradise Lost* only the devil and his followers are "heroic" in the old-fashioned epic style, but this is far indeed, as we have seen, from making them the heroes of the poem. Milton could not avoid using the War in Heaven (though he obviously had trouble with it), but he handles it so as to suggest that the end of all war is anarchy and indiscriminate destruction. In the vision of the future vouchsafed to Adam, the wars of history are wars against civilization, and when Satan, the dictator and demagogue, moves against Adam and Eve in Eden, he uses them as "things" in his war against God, though he has no personal malice against them, which is quite the way in which war-makers have always destroyed everybody and everything that stands in the way of their desired ends.

"And should I at your harmless innocence
Melt, as I do, yet public reason just,
Honor and empire with revenge enlarged
By conquering this new world, compels me now
To do what else though damned I should abhor."[31]

Of *Paradise Regained* we are told at the outset that it is "above heroic," and as the temptation develops Christ achieves a complete rejection of all non-spiritual means towards the achievement of spiritual ends, so much so as to give Tillyard the impression that Milton came to regret having supported the civil war. In Book I, Christ says that at one time he was tempted

"To rescue Israel from the Roman yoke,
Then to subdue and quell o'er all the earth
Brute violence and proud tyrannic power
Till truth was freed, and equity restored,"

but this feeling was succeeded by the realization, possibly derived from the Great Unknown Prophet of the Exile whose prophecies were bound up with those of Isaiah,

[31] Satan's resemblance to Iago is very close at this point, for Iago had no personal ill will toward Desdemona; he even "loved" her, much in the way that Satan "loves" Eve. Milton never forgot that peace can be corrupt as war, but perhaps we should remember that Iago too was a professional soldier!

"that my way must lie
Through many a hard assay even to the death,
Ere I the promised kingdom can attain,
Or work redemption for mankind, whose sins'
Full weight must be transferred upon my head."[32]

Satan advocates a militant Messianism to deliver Israel from the Roman yoke, but Christ uncompromisingly rejects it.

"They err who count it glorious to subdue
By conquest far and wide, to overrun
Large countries, and in field great battles win,
Great cities by assault. What do these worthies
But rob and spoil, burn, slaughter, and enslave
Peaceable nations, neighboring or remote,
Made captive, yet deserving freedom more
Than those their conquerors, who leave behind
Nothing but ruin, wheresoe'er they rove,
And all the flourishing works of peace destroy,
Then swell with pride, and must be titled gods,
Great benefactors of mankind, deliverers,
Worshipped with temple, priest, and sacrifice?"

Christ goes much further than this, however, condemning not only the conquerors but those who would resist them with their own weapons. He will not move against Tiberius as Judas Maccabeus moved against Antiochus, nor will he try to save Israel by playing off Rome against Parthia and Parthia against Rome. Thus the third book of *Paradise Regained* rejects *all* forms of military power, rejecting what we call "collective security" as well as what we call "aggression."[33]

[32] See John M. Steadman, "The 'Suffering Servant' and Milton's Heroic Norm," *HTR*, LIV (1961), 29–43, and cf. his *Milton's Epic Characters: Image and Idol* (University of North Carolina Press, 1968). Also see Merritt Y. Hughes, "The Christ of *Paradise Regained* and the Renaissance Heroic Tradition," *ELH*, XXXV (1938), 254–77; Frank Kermode, "Milton's Hero," *RES*, N.S. IV (1953), 317–30; Howard Schultz, "Christ and Antichrist in *Paradise Regained*," *PMLA*, LXVII (1952), 790–808.

[33] Reminding us that interest in astrology was widespread in England when *Paradise Regained* was written, with 1666 as a crucial year, Dick Taylor interprets

Was this, then, what Milton *believed* about war? It could not possibly be more than what he finally *came* to believe, for he wrote much that is not in harmony with it. The testimony of *Samson Agonistes* is tricky to invoke, since there is no complete agreement as to when that work was composed. If, however, it postdates *Paradise Regained*, I should have to say that if it does not quite consistently reinforce its predecessor, it involves no clear retractation either. I would not put much weight upon the consideration that Samson avenges himself upon his enemies by pulling down the Temple of Dagon upon them—and himself—for this was an inherited element in the story, and it would not have been possible for Milton to change it. The Christian ideal of the patient, long-suffering hero *is* present in *Samson Agonistes*, and the post-Biblical Samson tradition which (quite unreasonably, as it seems to us) had made Samson a type of Christ would make Milton's readers even more conscious of it than we are. And it must still be clear to even the most casual reader that the real blustering military hero of *Samson Agonistes* is not Samson but Harapha, who very likely descends from the *miles gloriosus* of Plautus and the braggart captains of Jonson and Beaumont and Fletcher.[34]

Until he lost his eyesight, Milton himself wore a sword and, we are told, prided himself upon his skill in using it, though I have no reason to suppose he ever pinked an adversary. Though he was sometimes bored by the military matters included in his *History of Britain*, he did not slight them, and he thought sports valuable because they contributed to the physical fitness which war demands. We have his own word for it that his aim in his tractate *Of Education* was to fit pupils "to perform justly, skilfully, and magnanimously all the offices both private and public of peace and war."[35] Finally it should be noted that in *Paradise Lost* itself,

---

even "The Storm Scene in *Paradise Regained*." *UTQ*, XXIV (1955), 359–76, as an attempt to persuade Christ through false portents that he should seize earthly power with Satan's help.

[34] See William O. Harris, "Despair and 'Patience as the Truest Fortitude' in *Samson Agonistes*," *ELH*, XXX (1963), 107–20, and, for the Samson tradition, F. Michael Krouse, *Milton's Samson and the Christian Tradition* (PUP, 1949). For Harapha consult Hughes, *Complete Poems and Major Prose*, pp. 535–36 and the references there cited.

though he says God was greater as creator than as conqueror of Satan, Milton does have God's forces, including his Son, employ force to conquer Satan, making use of the same kind of weapons as their adversaries, and even making the war more terrible than it would otherwise have been.[36]

Milton's most amazing statement about war is in the *Christian Doctrine*, where he tells us that since he could nowhere find it forbidden in the New Testament, he must regard it as quite as lawful now as it was in Bible times. Yet he must surely have known (for he could not have written *Paradise Regained* without knowing) that pacifist and non-pacifist notions concerning the nature of the Messiah existed in Israel. Did he miss the significance of the Palm Sunday procession, when Christ chose sides by riding into Jerusalem on an ass, the burden bearer of peace, rather than the war horse? Even if he did, *Paradise Regained* shows that he knew where Christ stood on this issue, and in his *Treatise on Civil Power*, he himself writes: "We read not that Christ ever exercised force but once; and that was to drive profane ones out of his Temple, not to force them in." Had Christ chosen the military,

---

[35] Hanford finds "the image of Milton practising the young Phillipses in the art of self-defence" a "very pleasant one." This depends entirely upon the taste and fancy of the imager, as Sam Weller might say, but when we find Hanford speaking of war as "this great and characteristic department of man's activity" and finding in it "a precious illustration in man of spiritual forces and of the triumph in human affairs of the almighty will" (which sounds a little like the perverted mysticism of a Hitler), we can hardly be surprised at his finding it so. When I taught at the University of Washington many years ago, at a time when some of us were trying to get rid of compulsory R.O.T.C., the *Daily* came out with an editorial in which Milton's words were quoted against us. This was a manifestation of literacy on the part of that newspaper to which we were unaccustomed, and I could not help wondering whether Milton's definition of education was the only thing I had taught the editors about him which had managed to stick. Another passage from *Paradise Lost* frequently quoted by militarists is Milton's reference to Belial, in Book II, ll. 227–28, as having "counseled ignoble ease, and peaceful sloth, / Not peace." They should observe the context more carefully. Belial is here open to criticism only on the ground that his motives are not pure. Under the conditions in which the fallen angels find themselves, what he advises is very sensible.

[36] C. S. Lewis insists that the war is not between Satan and Christ but between Satan and Michael, "and it is not so much won as stopped by Divine intervention." I fear this is not much more convincing than Mark Twain's honoring General Grant and Joan of Arc not so much for winning their wars as for ending them.

insurrectionist alternative, He would not have escaped the cross, but He would surely have won support against Rome from many zealots who, as it was, deserted him, and though we have no right to say that He was ever tempted by this alternative, He did know that it existed, and of this too Milton must have been fully aware.

Milton might properly reply to all this that if he tolerates war, it is only as other evils must be tolerated, in a fallen world, in which "true liberty / Is lost," and where man, having permitted

> "Within himself unworthy powers to reign
> Over free reason, God in judgment just
> Subjects him from without to violent lords;
> Who oft as undeservedly enthrall
> His outward freedom; tyranny must be,
> Though to the tyrant thereby no excuse."

As far as this defence goes, it is just, for it shows Milton's ability to see the whole moral spectrum and to keep its various sections in a proper relationship to each other. The puritan who calls an unchaste woman "bad," whatever other good qualities she may have, and a chaste woman "good," even though she may not possess a single other virtue, can never achieve more than a travesty of reasonable Christian ethics, and the pacifist who rejects and dissociates himself from war while remaining indifferent to all the evils of peace is no better. Yet when Tillyard attempts to enlarge upon this argument,[37] he seems to me to make a sorry mess of it.

> The nature of Adam's action [in deciding to sin along with Eve] can best be seen by the analogy of a man who hates war and yet consents to fight. To fight is bad, yet not to fight is worse because it is a denial of the common human fate, of an incrimination it is as yet impossible for any human being to be free of. To keep clear on narrowly personal moral grounds would be to incur a self-righteousness worse than the taint of association in an evil which all humanity is doomed to share.

Something of this every intelligent conscientious objector has

37 "The Crisis of *Paradise Lost*," in *Studies in Milton*.

felt, if only because his stand enables him to escape the sufferings which the soldier must bear. But the analogy is one of the worst on record and the reasoning based upon it is quite unconvincing. If we must fight because otherwise we shall feel self-righteous toward those who are fighting, why must we not commit all other sins deeply rooted in human nature lest we should vaunt ourselves upon these grounds? Chastity, sobriety, even kindness—is there no danger of self-righteousness here? All humanity is "doomed to share" the evil of war or any other evil whose cause and cure lies within the control of the human will only because most of us lack the moral backbone and independent thought and judgment which Tillyard found so dangerous to the life of the spirit. But I do not believe that any spiritually sensitive person is in danger of being engulfed by the feeling of self-righteousness for a moral victory which he has won on any particular issue; he will be all too painfully aware of the many issues upon which he has been defeated and of the many battles in other areas still waiting to be won. How well Tillyard knew the lives of the saints I have no idea, but he might have learned from them that they are of all men and women the most painfully conscious of their unworthiness. As for the insensitive, is their spiritual well-being really important enough so that we should be willing to support and preserve war as an institution in order to bolster it? In any case, the essential weakness of Milton's argument is his failure to distinguish between the Christian's *recognition* of the universality of sin since the Fall and the conviction that he, therefore, has a *right* to sin or that he is *commanded* to do evil for the sake of some hypothetical good, as every man under arms must, even in a "just" war.

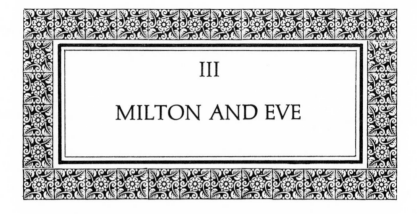

III

MILTON AND EVE

I

Milton was a passionate man of idealistic temperament and high moral principles; the combination is less rare than many persons imagine.

He was from youth [wrote William Vaughn Moody] more than ordinarily susceptible to the charm of women; boyishly, as we see in the first and seventh Latin elegies; with a youth's wistful expectancy, as in the Sonnet to the Nightingale; with a young man's chivalrous ardor, as in the Italian sonnets; and this susceptibility was greatly heightened by the austerity of a life which left the springs of concrete emotion untouched.

Certainly he was not cold; that would be difficult to postulate of such a lover of Ovid.

Elegy I, to Charles Diodati, is not very serious and specific.

. . . I do not let springtime pass by me in vain. I visit . . . a grove of close-set elms and a famous place of shade near the city. There you may often see groups of girls stroll by, stars that breathe out tempting flames, Ah, how many times have I stood transfixed by the marvelous beauty of a form that could restore youth even to old Jove! Ah, how many times have I seen eyes brighter than jewels and all the stars that both poles turn about, necks that surpass the arms of the twice-loving Pelops and the [Milky] Way that flows with pure nectar; and a glorious brow and waving hair, golden snares set by deceitful Love; alluring cheeks that make pallid the crimson of the hyacinth and the glow of even your flower, Adonis! Give way, you heroines so often praised of old, and every woman who captivated fickle Jove. . . . The prime glory belongs to British maidens; let it be enough for you, foreign women, to have second place.

Charming as this is, there is nothing much to say about it but that it expresses the pleasure that every normal young man must find in the sight of a pretty girl. But this particular young man is not yet ready to be taken, for he is not in love with a girl but only with love—and England! So we are not surprised when he concludes his panegyric as follows:

As for me, while the indulgence of the blind boy permits, I am preparing to depart with all speed from this fortunate city and, with the help of divine moly, to keep far from the infamous halls of the treacherous Circe. . . .

Only, it was not safe to twit "the blind boy." He would not always "permit."

The Fifth Elegy, written at twenty, though less personal, is more daring. The theme now is the quickening of the senses which spring brings to man and nature. The oread flees unwillingly from the wanton faun, hiding not too carefully lest she should fail to be found. The earth herself "breathes her amorous desires," voluptuously baring "her fertile bosom" and breathing out "the fragrance of Arabian harvests" while "from her lovely lips pours balsam and Paphian roses."

And throngs of girls go forth to enjoy the lovely spring, their maiden breasts girdled with gold. Every one has her own prayer, yet every one's is the same, that Cytherea may grant her the man of her desire.

The Sixth Elegy adds little beyond the admission that physical delights do inspire poetry of a kind (though not the kind that Milton wishes to write). But Elegy VII is another matter; now, for the first time, Milton is concerned not with *girls* but with *a girl*.

By chance I observed one who surpassed the others; that bright vision was the beginning of my pain. She looked as Venus herself might wish to appear to mortals; such to behold must the queen of the gods have been. It was that vengeful and wicked Cupid who had thrust her upon my sight; he alone wove this snare for me. Not far off the rascal himself was hiding, with his full quiver and his great torch hanging on his back. He did not delay. He clung now to the girl's eyelids, now to her face; then he alighted on her lips, then settled on her cheeks. And wherever the nimble archer fluttered, he wounded my defenceless breast—alas for me!—in a thousand places. All at once strange passions attacked my heart; I burned inwardly with love, I was all one flame.

There is no reason to doubt that this was an actual experience, but neither have we any reason to suppose that he ever saw her again. "Meanwhile she who alone charmed me had disappeared and left me dark, never again to return to my sight." It need not necessarily have been less precious for that; many a man has carried in his mind across a lifetime the memory of a face glimpsed but once. But if this is love of a kind, it is certainly not what most people mean by love; this Milton can hardly have known before he met the Emilia of the Italian sonnets.

It is not golden hair or a rosy cheek that so bewitches me, but a foreign beauty of a new pattern rejoices my heart—proud modesty of bearing, in her eyes that clear sheen of lovely black, speech adorned by more than one language, and a gift of song that might well drive the laboring moon astray in the middle of the sky, and from her eyes such a potent fire that wax in my ears would be of little use.

Sex, it seems, has proved stronger than patriotism, and "foreign women" have revenged themselves upon the vaunted "British maidens" of Elegy I.

We do not know much about this girl (even her given name is a comparatively recent discovery),[1] but she was cultured and of Italian origin (it is natural to conjecture that Milton may have met her through the Diodatis). How far their intimacy passed beyond the writing of sonnets on his part or how and why she passed out of his life we have no idea, but there is nothing to indicate that the experience left scars. Perhaps her nationality—and her special talent—prepared him for the ecstatic appreciation he was to pour out at the feet of a much greater singer, Leonora Baroni, when he was in Italy.

For your voice declares God's own presence. Either God or at least the third mind, quitting heaven, moves with secret power in your throat—moves with power, and graciously teaches mortal hearts how they can insensibly become accustomed to immortal sounds. But, if God is all things and interpenetrates all, in you alone he speaks, and in silence holds all else.

There speaks the idealistic lover of women indeed, for whom a woman cannot be beautiful without also being good and cannot sing like an angel without in a measure being one. (Adam did not go much further when, to Raphael's displeasure, he tried to find his standard in Eve.) And if Milton heard some of the gossip about Leonora that has filtered down to posterity, it is clear that he closed his mind to it, as idealistic young men always do under such circumstances.

Milton tells us specifically that as a young man he avoided the bordellos, and even if he did not tell us, we should be sure that this was true. Even books generally regarded as incitements to

[1] For what is known, or can reasonably be conjectured, see Parker, pp. 77–80, 744, 747–48, n. 6.

wantonness had no such effect on him, and he never affirmed his chastity save "to those who knew me not, for else it would be needless." Those Italians who did not admire his restraint were still impressed by it, and, as we have seen, his fellow Cantabrigians called him "the Lady of Christ's." The suggestion of weakness involved here made him indignant, and he proceeded to demonstrate conclusively that his language at least was not effeminate.

> But why do I seem to those fellows insufficiently masculine? . . . Doubtless it was because I was never able to gulp down huge bumpers in pancratic fashion; or because my hand has not become calloused by holding the plough-handle; or because I never lay down on my back under the sun at midday, like a seven-year ox-driver; perhaps, in fine, because I never proved myself a man in the same manner as those gluttons. But would that they could as easily lay aside their asshood as I whatever belongs to womanhood.[2]

He preferred even the austerity of Geneva to the profligacy of Naples, rejoicing that "in all these places where so much license is given I lived free and untouched of all defilement and profligate behavior, having it ever in my thought that if I could escape the eyes of men, I certainly could not escape the eyes of God." He nowhere mentions the sonnets which the Florentine Antonio Malatesti dedicated to him, very likely because he did not approve of their moral tone, and he was sure that "a certain reservedness of natural disposition and moral discipline learned out of the noblest philosophy" would have kept him abstemious even without religion.

---

[2] Was Milton ever guilty of obscenity? To a certain extent, yes, when he presided over the Cambridge revels, where it was expected of him, and again in the billingsgate with which he sometimes defiled his pamphlets. That his conscience was not wholly clear about this appears in the care with which he defends himself: one cannot describe vile things except in vile language; there is coarse language in the Bible; hypocrites condemn the words but would not shun the acts indicated. All of which, though true, does not quite cover the case. On certain aspects of Milton's attitude toward sexuality, see J. W. Saunders, "Milton, Diomede, and Amaryllis," *ELH*, XXII (1955), 254–86. But I do not find his dissent from the usual interpretation of the reference to Amaryllis in "Lycidas" quite convincing.

But having had the doctrine of Holy Scripture unfolding those chaste and high mysteries with timeliest care infused, that "the body is for the Lord and the Lord for the body," thus also I argued to myself, that if unchastity in a woman, whom Saint Paul terms the glory of man, be such a scandal and dishonor, then certainly in a man, who is both the image and glory of God, it must, though commonly not so thought, be much more deflowering and dishonorable, in that he sins both against his own body which is the perfecter sex, and his own glory which is in the woman, and that which is worst, against the image and glory of God which is in himself.

Stoll points out that even Milton's devils are not what might now (by the vulgar) be called "sexy." "Except in the story of the progeniture of Death, which is really no better than an allegory, there is little that is indecent or vicious about them." (Milton did, however, see the fallen angels as capable of lust, though not of love, and lust is an element in Satan's attitude toward Eve.) Except for physical hunger and the delicious smell of the "apple,"[3] the physical plays hardly any part in Milton's account of the Fall, though there is a riot of sensuality when he comes to describe the character and behavior of both Adam and Eve afterwards, and this contrast goes clear back to Saint Augustine. Sex has very little to do with Adam's decision to die with Eve. He is idolatrous, and uxorious in the extreme, but he is not impelled by fear of losing the ecstasies of copulation but rather (and this is quite in harmony with Milton's own emphasis in his divorce pamphlets) of the loneliness he must face in the "wild woods forlorn." Stoll contrasts Milton in this aspect with Dante, whose devils have much more "naughty ways and indecorous demeanor," and the contrast appears again in Milton's "grand spaciousness and Tintorettesque chiaroscuro," where Dante "dwells on the stench [of hell] in true mediaeval fashion; and the various tortures are so exactly and relentlessly described as often to be grotesque or revolting."

[3] In early English, "apple" is a generic term for fruit, just as "deer" indicates animals. As Milton describes the forbidden fruit, it seems much more like a peach than what we should call an apple.

The most passionate glorification of chastity in Milton's early work lies in Comus, where it appears notably in the Elder Brother's conviction that "virtue may be assailed, but never hurt," and that his sister, possessing it, is "clad in cómplete steel," and even more in the great debate between Comus and the Lady which begins in line 665. There have been solemn debates in the learned journals as to whether Milton ever changed his mind about chastity, whether or not he equated it with continence, and whether Comus was or was not altered to correspond to his altered views.[4] Surely J. C. Maxwell is right both when he declares that "there is enough great poetry that is difficult to interpret without our creating difficulties in works which are essentially simple" and again when he points out that "at various stages virtue reveals itself in different contexts, as chastity, as virginity, as temperance, as continence." Of course the Lady's chastity is a spiritual matter, and something much greater than mere physical virginity. But at her time of life it would certainly embrace physical virginity. The role was played by the daughter of the Earl of Bridgewater, and though a seventeenth-century poet would probably not have had his head chopped off for being fool enough to cause a nobleman's fifteen-year-old daughter and her brothers to raise questions about her virginity in an entertainment presented in her father's honor, one could hardly argue that he did not deserve it.[5] The Lady's

[4] See E. M. W. Tillyard, Essays and Studies, XXVIII (1942), 22–37; Kenneth Muir, Penguin New Writing, XXIV (1945), 141–43; J. C. Maxwell, "The Pseudo-Problem of Comus," Cambridge Journal, I (1947–48), 376–80. Rose Macaulay's little book on Milton is in many respects charming, but it contains two passages which one can hardly believe were written by a sane woman. In one she declares that "On the Late Massacre in Piedmont" is not a very good sonnet. In the other, she finds Comus "the most attractive being in Milton's repertory, except possibly the jocund hero of 'L'Allegro.' There is a spirit and grace about him, inherited from his two charming parents. . . ." Divine grace, perhaps. Especially from his mother, that delightful ingénue, Circe. Truly, de gustibus non. . . .

[5] The following lines do not appear in the Bridgewater Manuscript; Parker conjectures that perhaps they may have been considered unfit to be spoken in the presence of the Lady Alice:

"List, lady, be not coy, and be not cozened
With that same vaunted name Virginity;
Beauty is Nature's coin, must not be hoarded,
But must be current, and the good thereof

attitude toward marriage, at some time in the future, if she had one, was no part of the problem with which either she or Milton now had to deal. Comus does not propose marriage to her, and we need not stop to speculate about what would have happened if he had. If he had, he would not have been Comus, and the masque would not have been *Comus* either, but what Kipling calls "another story." We need not study the poem Milton did not write; we shall have enough to do understanding what he did write. To assume that we know, from this work, either that the Lady will sometime marry or that she will not is quite unwarranted. As Maxwell says, the question does not arise. What *is* important is that she is now a chaste girl. And if she does some day marry, she will become a chaste wife also.

In any case, it would be difficult to show that Milton at any time overvalued continence.[6] In his youth, before he had any prospects, he looked forward to a "house and family of his own." He was still planning to be a priest when he wrote this; he would have been a strange sort of Puritan if he had thought of celibacy as a requirement for priests,[7] and it should not be forgotten that he thought of himself as a kind of priest even after he had changed his plans. It is true that he did not marry young—studious, fastidious young men often do not—but if he anywhere shows the influence of Spenser it is in the high regard he expresses for marriage, contrasting sharply with both the Court of Love ideas that were undergoing a renascence in his time and the vulgar satires of popular literature. We have already considered what Rajan calls his "overwhelming awareness of fertility" in *Paradise Lost*. If he is "Puritanical" about it, this is because he was aware of what moderns are in considerable danger of forgetting, "that fertility

Consists in mutual and partaken bliss,
Unsavory in th'enjoyment of itself.
If you let slip time, like a neglected rose
It withers on the stalk with languished head."

[6] The principal argument to the contrary is that of Ernest Sirluck, "Milton's Idle Right Hand," *JEGP*, LX (1961), 749–85, but it is not convincing. See Parker, pp. 800–801.

[7] William R. Haller, "Hail, Wedded Love," *ELH*, XIII (1946), 79–97, and (with Malleville Haller), "The Puritan Art of Love," *HLQ*, V (1942), 235–72.

is made possible, and not merely assisted by, restraint." ("Milton refuses to sport with Amaryllis," says Rajan, "because it is ordinary good sense to prefer Urania.") He would not praise "a fugitive and cloistered virtue, unexercised and unbreathed." Like Spenser, again (and like all good Platonists), he shunned both libertinism and asceticism, accepting and enjoying all the good things of this world as so many expressions or manifestations of an immaterial spiritual good behind them which informs them and which brought them into being. He would not have been surprised to learn that a great many of the persons who have made sex an important element in their art have been undersexed rather than oversexed in their private lives, nor yet that it would be extremely difficult for a really lewd woman to become what is now called a "sex symbol." And there is at least one interesting passage in the divorce pamphlets which might well be pondered by those who believe that the dangers of repression were never realized before Freud:

Let not therefore the frailty of man go on thus inventing needless troubles to itself, to groan under the false imagination of a strictness never imposed from above, enjoining that for duty which is an impossible and vain supererogating. "Be not righteous overmuch," is the counsel of Ecclesiastes; "why shouldst thou destroy thyself?" Let us not be thus overcurious to strain at atoms, and yet to stop every vent and cranny of permissive liberty, lest nature, wanting those needful pores and breathing-places which God hath not debarred our weakness, either suddenly break out into some wide rupture of open vice, and frantic heresy, or else inwardly fester with repining and blasphemous thoughts.

If this passage were included in a series of extracts from English writers requiring identification in an examination, how many students would assign it to Milton? Not many, I venture. Yet nobody can claim to understand him who would find the ascription impossible.

II

Milton uses sexual figures when they apply ("one fellow rails foolishly at Dialectic, which he never will be able to comprehend; another regards Philosophy as of no value, because, forsooth, Nature, most beautifully formed of the goddesses, has never deemed him worthy of such an honor that she would permit him to gaze upon her naked") and allows the marriage of the Lamb in Revelation to prompt him to describe the apotheosis of Lycidas in terms not uncolored with sexual ecstasy.[8] In *Paradise Lost* Eve's nakedness is as lovingly described as any Renaissance painter ever pictured it.

> She as a veil down to the slender waist
> Her unadorned golden tresses wore
> Disheveled, but in wanton ringlets waved
> As the vine curls her tendrils. . . .

Moreover Milton goes out of his way to insist that both she and Adam went with their private parts uncovered, and that they used them, joyfully, for the purpose for which they had been designed.

> Nor those mysterious parts were then concealed;
> Then was not guilty shame; dishonest shame
> Of Nature's works, honor dishonorable,
> Sin-bred, how have ye troubled all mankind
> With shows instead, mere shows of seeming pure,
> And banished from man's life his happiest life,

---

[8] I first encountered Milton through "L'Allegro" and "Il Penseroso" in a fourth-year high school course in English. This was long before high school teachers had taken upon themselves the noble task of opening the minds of their pupils by introducing them to such writers as D. H. Lawrence and Henry Miller, while as for Ernest Hemingway, he was one of my classmates. It still amuses me to remember how shocked some of the boys were by the sexual references at the beginning of both poems, never having encountered anything like this before in literature read in school. I can still hear them say, "And him a Puritan!" I offer these reminiscences merely as a quaint footnote to the cultural (or, if the reader prefer, anti-cultural) history of America. This was the same period when, as Lillian Gish has recently revealed, D. W. Griffith was shocked by Marguerite Clark (of all innocent actresses!) because, in one scene of her first film, *Wildflower*, she took off her stockings on the screen. How, he asked, could he compete with something like that?

Simplicity and spotless innocence.
So passed they naked on, nor shunned the sight
Of God or angel, for they thought no ill;
So hand in hand they passed, the loveliest pair
That ever since in love's embraces met.

This, moreover, is exactly what God intends.

Whatever hypocrites austerely talk
Of purity and place and innocence,
Defaming as impure what God declares
Pure, and commands to some, leaves free to all.
Our Maker bids increase; who bids abstain
But our destroyer, foe to God and man?

Nor is it only before Adam that Eve is shameless. When
Raphael comes to dinner,

Eve
Undecked save with herself, more lovely fair
Than wood-nymph, or the fairest goddess feigned
Of three that in Mount Ida naked strove,
Stood to entertain her guest from heav'n; no veil
She needed, virtue-proof, no thought infirm
Altered her cheek.

And again:

Meanwhile at table Eve
Ministered naked, and their flowing cups
With pleasant liquors crowned. O innocence
Deserving Paradise! If ever, then,
Then had the Sons of God excuse to have been
Enamored at that sight; but in those hearts
Love unlibidinous reigned, nor jealousy
Was understood, the injured lover's hell.

Before Raphael's visit has been concluded, Adam specifically
asks him,

"Love not the heav'nly Spirits, and how their love
Express they, by looks only, or do they mix
Irradiance, virtual or immediate touch?"

and though this brings the Angel

a smile that glowed
Celestial rosy red, love's proper hue,

he answers directly enough, and what his answer amounts to is
that if men and women copulate, angels super-copulate. They have
no genitalia; instead they interpenetrate each other completely,
so that in a way their whole being is an organ of copulation. To
their pleasure there is no "obstacle . . . of membrane, joint, or
limb."

"Easier than air with air, if Spirits embrace,
Total they mix, union of pure with pure
Desiring; nor restrained conveyance need
As flesh to mix with flesh, or soul with soul."

Copulation in Eden was not original with Milton; Albertus
Magnus declared that man would have enjoyed much greater
sexual pleasure if he had not lost Paradise. Milton does stress it,
however, rejecting the other tradition that the marriage of Adam
and Eve was not consummated until after the Fall,[9] and he had
a sounder metaphysical basis both for this and for his beliefs about
angels[10] than many others possessed because he did not make the

---

[9] See Frank Kermode, "Adam Unparadised," in his edited anthology, *The
Living Milton*, especially pp. 103 ff.

[10] The standard account of Milton's angelology is Robert H. West, *Milton and
the Angels* (University of Georgia Press, 1955). See also his article, "Milton's
Angelogical Heresies," *JHI*, XIV (1953), 116–22, and cf. E. L. Marilla's "Milton
on Conjugal Love among the Heavenly Angels," in his *Milton & Modern Man*.
Aquinas says angels are attracted to each other but does not have them express
their love by caresses or penetration. Henry More thought they could penetrate
each other's substance as well as penetrating matter, but he does not suggest that
there is anything amorous in such penetration. It is interesting that neither the
amorousness nor the angels' power of digestion appears in *Christian Doctrine*,
which suggests that Milton did not regard it as deducible from the Bible nor
"believe" in it in the sense in which he believed in what he regarded as fundamental
Christian doctrines.

sharp distinction between matter and spirit which most Christians have made. The conventional belief that spirit is "good" and matter—or flesh—"evil" can hardly be erected upon such a foundation. Furthermore, Milton was a traducianist, which means that he did not believe that parents create the bodies of their children while God himself creates each fresh soul by an "immediate act"; he believed rather that soul and body are generated or propagated together, and that the divine blessing is "no less efficacious in imparting to man the power of producing after his kind, than to the other parts of animated nature." On this basis, intercourse for the purpose of procreation becomes "creative" in a far more spiritual sense than many persons, even many Christians, think of it as being, even today.

As I have already suggested, however, Milton does insist upon a sharp difference between sex before the Fall and after it. If there is no nobler description of intercourse in literature than his of the union of Adam and Eve before the Fall, there is nothing much uglier than his account of what they do at the end of Book IX, after they have sinned. C. S. Lewis believed that the first was much less precisely indicated than the second because, being himself a fallen man, writing for fallen men and women, Milton did not really know anything about unfallen sexuality. In the absolute sense this is no doubt quite true. But he must have known—or, being a poet, he must easily have been able to imagine—the difference between noble and ignoble sexuality even in our world, in other words, between sex involving two people who respect themselves and each other, and who are drawn together by their mutual love and desire for oneness, and that sex in which each party "uses" the other only for its own unreasoned sensual gratification, regardless of all the other ends and duties of life, and with no hesitation about victimizing the partner in order to secure it. This is essentially the contrast Milton develops. Because shame and guilt have appeared after the Fall, pleasure itself has been diminished; as St. Thomas Aquinas says, "a sober person does not take less pleasure in food taken in moderation than the glutton." Passion has now become destructive; it befuddles the understanding, and both parties behave exactly as if they were drunk.

As with new wine intoxicated both
They swim in mirth, and fancy that they feel
Divinity within them breathing wings
Wherewith to scorn the earth.

If they still need each other, it is only for gratification of their own passions. Adam now "loves" Eve in the sense in which the cat "loves" the mouse, and he achieves much the same kind of union with her, for the destruction of the weaker party is the logical outcome of the "love" whose passion is unmodified by either tenderness or respect. Nor is she any better, for, once fallen, she gave him to eat because she would rather have him die with her than live, however happily or sinlessly, without her. (The vicious are always more scornful of the virtues of others than the narrowest puritan has ever been of their vices.) And it is not the least tragic element in their situation that, now having come to the place where they have lost everything except each other, they should find that gone too and turn to ignoble bickering. Unwilling to admit her fault and shoulder her own share of the responsibility, Eve blames Adam himself for her fall: he ought not, she says, to have permitted her to go away from him![11] As for Adam, he knows

[11] Some of Milton's commentators join her in blaming Adam for this. "Go," he finally says to her, having demolished all her sophistries to no avail, "Go; for thy stay, not free, absents thee more." Yet he treats her exactly as God treats him and all mankind. If she was inferior to Adam, she was still a human being, with all a human being's right to freedom. And surely the difference between her and Adam was infinitely less than that between Adam and God. She, however, is restless, rebellious, "unbuxom," and, insofar as such qualities could be manifested before the Fall, a little vulgar. Unmindful of her weakness, overconfident (as the event proves) of her stability, she is willing, even eager, to expose herself to a temptation from which a more delicate sensibility would have shrunk. As Sir Thomas Overbury was to put it,

In part to blame is she,
Which hath without consent been only tried;
He comes too near that comes to be denied.

Another mistake about Eve is made by those who argue that Milton must have sympathized with her because he permits her to use some of the same arguments

that he has sinned, but, not unreasonably as it must now appear to the fallen, selfish, self-centered mind which is all he has left himself to reason with, he feels that she for whom his sin was committed ought to be the last to blame him for it. And so harmony and sin cannot co-exist, even for those who sin together. Adam can die for Eve, but she can never again be to him what once she was. There is no honor among thieves and no peace among the wicked, not because God has arbitrarily decreed it so but because it is the nature of vice and crime to destroy peace and honor.

But although all this is true, there is a related proposition, the bearings of which are not always clearly perceived, but which is still more significant for the understanding of Milton's mind. Adam's sin was idolatry, uxoriousness, and weakness. Adam chose Eve, the lesser good, instead of the infinitely greater good which is God, and when he decided, in an instant, that he could not live without her, he was making God nothing. Christ spells all this out very carefully when He comes to the garden in judgment:

"Was she thy God, that her thou didst obey
Before his voice, or was she made thy guide,
Superior, or but equal, that to her
Thou didst resign thy manhood, and the place
Wherein God set thee above her, made of thee
And for thee, whose perfection far excelled
Hers in all real dignity?"

But note how carefully He goes on to explain that the fault was not in Eve as wife or woman but simply in Adam, who did not choose the bad but misused the good:

---

he used in the *Areopagitica*. John S. Diekhoff, "Eve, the Devil, and the *Areopagitica*," *Modern Language Quarterly*, V (1944), 429–34, has unanswerably pointed out that these persons ignore the world of differences between the two situations involved. Milton wrote the *Areopagitica* for men inhabiting a fallen world, where good and evil grow up together and man must, through experience and experimentation, learn to distinguish and choose between them. But Eve was in Paradise. All that was asked of her was obedience.

"Adorned
She was indeed, and lovely to attract
Thy love, not thy subjection, and her gifts
Were such as under government well seemed,
Unseemly to bear rule, which was thy part
And person, hadst thou known thy self aright."

Another passage, in Book X, seems to me even more remarkable. Adam and Eve are discussing the possibility of saving mankind from God's curse by refusing to propagate. She is not sure that they could achieve it.

"But if thou judge it hard and difficult,
Conversing, looking, loving, to abstain
From love's due rights, nuptial embraces sweet,
And with desire to languish without hope,"

why, then, let them kill themselves too. So, even now, what the Fall has left them of the ecstasies of copulation is the chief blessing of life!

III

Concerning Milton's own experience of matrimony we know much less than we should like to know. He was married three times—to Mary Powell in 1642, to Katherine Woodcock in 1656, and to Elizabeth Minshull in 1663. By Mary Powell he had four children: Anne (b. July, 1646); Mary (b. October, 1648); John (b. March, 1651), Milton's only son, who died in 1652, Edward Phillips says, "through the ill usage, or bad conditioning, of an ill-chosen nurse"; and Deborah (b. 1652). His only child by his second marriage, Katherine (b. 1657), lived only five months, and he had no issue by Elizabeth Minshull. Mary Powell died in 1652, at the age of twenty-seven, a few days after Deborah's birth, and Katherine Woodcock on February 3, 1658, a month and fourteen days before the death of the child she had borne on October 18. Elizabeth Minshull outlived the poet.

We know little about Milton's relations with Katherine Woodcock. If we are to take the sonnet "Methought I saw my late espousèd saint" (XXIII), as it has generally been taken, as Milton's tribute to her, then either the relationship was idyllic or Milton greatly idealized her in retrospect. Parker has argued[12] that it applies instead to Mary Powell, but he does not seem to have made many converts. Elizabeth Minshull, whom Milton called "Betty," seems to have been a good, kind, motherly woman, who looked after her blind husband's creature comforts and took the best possible care of him, but I sense a certain condescension in such references to her as have been preserved, and I would guess that, like many quite "satisfactory" unions formed late in the husband's life, the success of this one rested mainly upon a practical basis.

Not that it would have been reasonable for a man like Milton to expect to find a wife who was his intellectual equal. How many such women were alive in the seventeenth century? Certainly Mary Powell was not his equal, yet she may well have been the love of his life, for all that. Certainly she is the wife who has interested posterity most. Let Edward Phillips tell as much of the story as he can:

About Whitsuntide it was, or a little after, that he took a journey into the country; nobody about him certainly knowing the reason, or that it was any more than a journey of recreation; after a month's stay, home he returns a married man, that went out a bachelor; his wife being Mary, the eldest daughter of Mr. Richard Powell, then a justice of peace, of Foresthill, near Shotover in Oxfordshire; some few of her nearest relations accompanying the bride to her new habitation. . . . At length they took their leave and returning to Foresthill left the sister behind, probably not much to her satisfaction as appeared by the sequel. By that time she had for a month or thereabout led a philosophical life (after having been used to a great house, and much company and joviality), her friends, possibly incited by her own desire, made earnest suit by letter, to have her company

[12] *Milton*, pp. 475–76, 1045, n. 145.

the remaining part of the summer, which was granted, on condition of her return at the time appointed, Michaelmas or thereabout. . . .

Michaelmas being come, and no news of his wife's return, he sent for her by letter; and receiving no answer, sent several other letters, which were also unanswered; so that at last he dispatched down a foot messenger with a letter, desiring her return. But the messenger came back not only without an answer, at least a satisfactory one, but in the best of my remembrance, reported that he was dismissed with some sort of contempt. This proceeding in all probability was grounded upon no other cause but this, namely, that the family being generally addicted to the cavalier party, as they called it, and some of them possibly engaged in the King's service, who by this time had his headquarters at Oxford, and was in some prospect of success, they began to repent them of having matched the eldest daughter of the family to a person so contrary to them in opinion; and thought it would be a blot in their escutcheon, whenever that court should come to flourish again.

However, it so incensed our author that he thought it would be dishonorable ever to receive her again, after such a repulse; so that he forthwith prepared to fortify himself with arguments for such a resolution, and accordingly wrote two [sic] treatises, by which he undertook to maintain, that it was against reason, and the enjoinment of it not provable by Scripture, for any married couple disagreeable in humor and temper, or having an aversion to each other, to be forced to live yoked together all their days. . . .

There has been much speculation as to *why* Milton married Mary Powell. Such speculation is generally silly, and this is more than commonly so. One would think some scholars had never heard of marriage, that they are driven to such fantastic lengths as speculating upon the possibility of the bride having been used to pay off a debt which the Powells owed Milton's father![13] Milton

---

[13] It might be added that the hypothesis of Saurat and others, that the marriage

married Mary Powell because she was a girl of seventeen and pretty and he was a man approaching his mid-thirties who was strongly attracted by women but had hitherto had very little to do with them in an intimate way. For whatever reason he visited the Powells, he must have been brought into closer relations with Mary than he had ever been with any other eligible girl. If he had *not* fallen in love with her, there would be some excuse for our head-scratching; as it is, there is none.

We no longer believe with Masson that *The Doctrine and Discipline of Divorce* was on sale virtually before Milton's honeymoon was over, for we now have good reason to date the marriage a year earlier than he did. Nevertheless, the position he staked out —which was, briefly, that divorce should be permitted, upon the fiat of the contracting parties themselves, for what we call "incompatibility of temper"—was very daring for the time. Nor would he have kept the thing wholly in the realm of theory, for we are told that he was "in treaty" concerning marriage with another woman when Mary suddenly forestalled him by coming back into his life. There is no reason to suppose that, had this not occurred, he would not have attempted to carry through the plan, though the "averseness" of the lady in question, "one of Dr. Davis's daughters, a very handsome and witty gentlewoman," was, of course, a slight handicap, (Nobody has ever called poor Mary "witty.") Perhaps Dr. Davis' daughter was not attracted by the idea of running the risk of an accusation of bigamy, the laws of England relating to that subject being what they were.

To what extent rumors of such contemplated action were bruited about, and if so whether they alarmed Mary, we do not know, but she did take the initiative that resulted in reconciliation, or permitted it to be taken in her behalf. One day, when Milton was visiting his friends and hers, the Blackboroughes, he found her waiting for him in an adjoining room. . . .

The pretty legend that Milton was recalling this scene when he wrote the passage in *Paradise Lost* in which a weeping, repent-

---

was never consummated until after Mary's return to Milton, is wholly unsubstantiated.

ant Eve comes to Adam after the Fall is just that, but we do know that she implored his forgiveness and blamed her mother for what the seventeenth century might have called her unbuxomness, and everything we know about Mrs. Powell inclines us to believe that Mary was telling the truth.

And, of course, we know one thing more—that Milton forgave her. Despite all the brave words he had written about being yoked to an image of phlegm and the degradation involved in preserving a union of bodies where no union of minds might be achieved, he forgave her, and there was no thought of Miss Davis or any other woman in his life while Mary was alive.

"Yet beauty, though injurious, hath strange power,
After offense returning, to regain
Love once possessed, nor can be easily
Repulsed, without much inward passion felt
And secret sting of amorous remorse."

Why is it that the persons who are so eager to quote whatever in Milton's writings might be made to redound to the discredit of Mary Powell never quote these lines from *Samson Agonistes* which seem to favor her?

Did he love her? and was the marriage thereafter a happy one? I think there can be no doubt about the first question. It is very unlikely that Milton had ever stopped loving Mary Powell; had he done so, her desertion would not have wounded him so much. One may suppose that he must very early have learned that there were vast areas in the deeper reaches of his being that he could never share with this girl, but he was not the kind of man who, having once given his heart, could take it back again without tearing up the roots of his being. There is nothing to indicate that he ever had any doubt concerning the soundness of anything he had written in the divorce pamphlets, but from 1645 on none of this any longer applied to him. Divorce had ceased to be a personal issue. Surely this could not have happened if love had died.

As to how happy—or unhappy—they were together, we simply do not know. Is there a perfectly happy marriage or a perfectly happy anything else in this world? Had Mary—a woman now, not a girl—changed since she had left him? Milton certainly had not changed, nor was he ever to do so; neither did he alter his way of life; when Mary came back to live with him, it must have been she who altered hers. Did she do this willingly, pulling herself out of her mother's orbit and into her husband's because she knew now that there was where she belonged and wanted to be? And did she live thereafter, a happy young wife and mother, until she died? If we could be sure that Parker was right in making "Methought I saw" apply to her, the argument for this hypothesis would be greatly strengthened, but I fear we cannot be sure. At least let us say that we *know* of no further strife between them. It is *possible* that Milton may have intended to embrace her in his strictures upon her noisy, inconsiderate family, when, fallen upon evil days, they took refuge in his house, but it is not *necessary* to believe this. Unless she was a cretin, she must have known that her husband behaved very generously when he gave her uncongenial family refuge, and unless she was a clod, she must have been aware of the tension that existed in her household while her family inhabited it, but if she was by this time firmly on her husband's side, the strain on the marriage tie was greatly lessened. There is also the slighting reference to the "undutiful children" he had by her in Milton's will, but though this does not seem to imply much tenderness toward her, it is not directed against her personally, and she had long been dead when it was made. We may feel that he wore her out with childbearing and buried her at twenty-seven, but the intervals between the first two births at least were very reasonable by seventeenth-century standards.[14]

The daughters, of course, lived on. The eldest, Anne, though attractive to see, was apparently "retarded" and not quite able-bodied. None of them seem to have had much gift for letters, and Milton, apparently despairing of anything better for them, finally

[14] The scholarly Victorian novelist Anne Manning (1807–79) wrote *The Maiden and Married Life of Mary Powell* (1849) and *Deborah's Diary* (1859), supplying journals both for Milton's wife and her youngest daughter. These are spare, beautiful, restrained works of art. Robert Graves's much more recent *Wife to Mr. Milton* (1943) is a savage attack on the poet.

spent a good deal of money to have them learn a "gentlewomanly" trade. Anne signed the receipt for her share of his estate with a mark, and Mary spelled Milton with a small *m* and two *l*'s. Yet Richardson says that Milton would call his daughters at any hour of the night to take down what came to him! Even a girl who understood the value of what her father was creating would have had to be something close to a saint to be willing to make such sacrifices for it—and him—and there is no indication that Milton's daughters did understand; they were no part of that "fit audience though few" for which he labored. Edward Phillips adds that his uncle required both the younger girls to read to him in his blindness in "Hebrew (and I think the Syriac), the Greek, the Latin, Spanish, and French," and one does not know whether to marvel more at his ability to understand what to them must have been so much gibberish or at their patience to go through with it.[15] Patience, according to the legend, had little to do with the matter, and Munkácsy's immense canvas of Milton dictating *Paradise Lost* to his daughters, which hangs over the staircase in the New York Public Library, fairly crackles with hatred and resentment, never remotely suggesting that anybody pictured in it has the remotest concern with spiritual matters.[16] Nor do the daughters seem to have taken kindly to the third wife.

Like most men of means in his time, Milton was accustomed to personal services from his youth. Aubrey says that, as a child, when he studied until midnight or after, "his father ordered the maid to sit up for him," and it does not seem to have occurred to either of these males that this was an unreasonable imposition upon a woman who had probably been working all day and who must get up early in the morning to begin her work again.

Yet Milton's relations with his daughters may not have been

[15] Was Phillips' report, like that of Mark Twain's death, greatly exaggerated? How did these unschooled girls learn how to pronounce the Greek and Hebrew characters? And how could their blind father have taught them this?

[16] How different this is from the eyewitness description of Milton, in his later years, dictating, leaning back in his chair, and with one leg flung carelessly across the arm! But this would not harmonize with the Roman senator conception which most people who know nothing about him have of Milton.

quite so uncomfortable as we have sometimes assumed. We have, to be sure, the shocking story that when Mary heard he was to marry Elizabeth Minshull, she remarked that the news of his wedding could not interest her much, but that if she could hear that he was dead, that would be worth hearing, and the same servant who testifies to this adds that Milton's children conspired with tradespersons to cheat him and tried to sell his books away from him for waste paper. But the testimony of servants is not always reliable, and over against this we must place the account of Deborah's emotion when Jonathan Richardson showed her the Faithorne crayon of Milton: " 'Tis my father! 'Tis my dear father! I see him! 'Tis him!" Richardson says too that Deborah spoke of her father

> with great tenderness: particularly I have been told she said he was delightful company, the life of the conversation, and that on account of a flow of subject and an unaffected cheerfulness and civility.

Perhaps Deborah, being the "baby," had felt Milton's severity less than her sisters. She was the only one of the girls who wanted any mementoes—or anything else than money—from his estate. We hear of his having tried to teach her Latin, and in her later years she herself did some teaching. Perhaps she left home when she did against his will, and it may be that by the time the estate was settled, her resentment had been softened by time or even replaced by remorse.

IV

Richard Garnett declared that Milton's "he for God only, she for God in him" embodied "every fallacy concerning woman's relation to her husband and to her Maker." So it must seem to a feminist age. Says Eve,

> "I chiefly who enjoy
> So far the happier lot, enjoying thee
> Pre-eminent by so much odds, while thou
> Like consort to thyself canst nowhere find,"

and again,

> "My author and disposer, what thou bidd'st
> Unargued I obey; so God ordains.
> God is thy law, thou mine; to know no more
> Is woman's happiest knowledge and her praise."

Adam stands as a kind of high priest between her and God, and though she does not lack intelligence, she would rather learn from him at second hand than from Raphael directly. Douglas Bush has rightly observed that she thinks about her husband much more than she thinks about God, and when they are expelled from the Garden together, Adam laments the loss of divine communion while she mourns the loss of her flowers and her home. But if Milton thought this made her inferior to Adam (and, by implication, women inferior to men), he did not blame her for it. This was the way God made it and the way it ought to be, and whatever was, was right. There was nothing about any of this that was peculiar to Milton. He shared these notions with the whole tradition of Hebrew-Christian civilization, and he could not have denied them without flying in the face of that tradition, violating the principle of order, and breaking the Great Chain of Being.[17] Nobody who knows him will need to be told that he would have done just that had such action seemed to him to be called for. He did not so conceive it. But where he does depart from conventional ideas, it is always because he sympathizes more with women than other men did, not less.

Milton's condemnation of Adam for the sin of idolatry in choosing Eve before God shows that he never accepted the extreme romantic view that love is the supreme good of life.[18] ("You cannot devote your life to two divinities," says Bernard Shaw, "God and the person you are married to.") He praised Dante and Petrarch for showing respect to the women they loved, but he

---

[17] See E. M. W. Tillyard, *The Elizabethan World Picture* (CW, 1943); Marjorie Nicolson, *The Breaking of the Circle* (ColUP, 1960); and, for a brief statement, Nicolson, *Reader's Guide*, pp. 25–52.

[18] See Paul Turner, "Woman and the Fall of Man," *English Studies*, XXIX (1948), 1–18.

had no sympathy with the courtly love tradition which placed woman upon an unnatural and unrealistic eminence, and in *Paradise Lost* he had Satan approach Eve like a courtly love poet. Platonic love, which had experienced a late revival at the court of Queen Henrietta Maria, aroused no sympathy in him either. He did not believe in its vaunted "purity," but since he despised both libertinism and asceticism, he would not have valued it much more if he had so believed. Though Milton did not always escape the innocence of the unworldly, every now and then he surprises us by his insight into human temptations. "No man knows hell like him who converses most in heaven," and certainly Milton had no delusions as to "spiritual" people being free from danger. If he could have witnessed an American frontier revival of "power" (which is a trial he was fortunately spared), I doubt that he would have been surprised to find the bushes well filled. For all this, no romantic could have presented Adam's dilemma more understandingly; if our judgment is never befuddled, we still have to struggle to keep our hearts from taking his part. Milton opposed forced or "arranged" loveless marriages, which were very widely accepted in his time, and he seems to have intended that men and women should enjoy equal rights of divorce. He demanded the same chastity of men that society at large required of women, and he decisively rejected the common Renaissance notion that companionship between man and woman stood on a lower level than that between man and man.[19] If he had not entertained a flatteringly high opinion of women, he certainly could not have desired spiritual and intellectual communion with them as he did. A contemporary critic once complained that

> we believe you to count no woman to due conversation accessible as to you, except she can speak Hebrew, Greek, Latin and French, and dispute against the Canon Law as well as you, or at least be able to hold discourse with you.

This, of course, is an absurd exaggeration; when Milton speaks of

[19] See A. H. Gilbert, "Milton on the Position of Women," *Modern Language Review*, XV (1920), 17–27, 240–64.

"conversation" in marriage, he is not using the word in its modern sense; what he desires is the harmonious adjustment of personalities and communion of soul with soul. Walter Bagehot, though much less serious, comes closer to the mark when he observes that while many men have claimed that women talked too much, only Milton wanted them to talk more![20] Whatever else male superiority may have involved, it did not, then, in theory at least, involve riding rough-shod over the woman, for Eve is not merely Adam's helpmate; God himself calls her his other self. "The woman ought in such wise to be loved as the Church is beloved of Christ, for it was man's greatest honor that a creature so much like him as woman should be subordinated to him."

All this appears clearly in the very area where its presence has been most often denied—that is to say, in the divorce pamphlets. Milton, as I have already said, advocated divorce for incompatibility of temper, and because he saw marriage as a civil contract, not a sacrament, he gave the church little to do in connection with it.[21] One can easily understand how this must have seemed moral anarchy to his contemporaries, or even how some persons might be shocked by it in the much freer society of today, but there is no excuse for any intelligent person who fails to recognize that it was his fundamentally spiritual view of marriage which compelled him to regard spiritual shortcomings and deficiencies as more destructive of the marriage relationship than even adultery itself, which, indeed, he once bluntly calls an "accident." For

> God in the first ordaining of marriage taught us to what end he did it, in words expressly implying the apt and cheerful conversation of man with woman, to comfort and refresh him against the evil of solitary life, not mentioning the purpose of generation till afterwards, as being but a secondary end in dignity, though not in necessity. . . .

In other words, the sexual basis of marriage was boldly accepted, but when copulation was unaccompanied by the union of souls,

[20] *Literary Studies,* Vol. I (Longmans, Green, 1879).
[21] For the procedure, see Parker, *Milton,* pp. 243–44.

it seemed to Milton indistinguishable from the coupling of cattle. Intercourse without pleasure, for generation only, was as degrading as lust itself, and nothing could be more horrible than "to grind in the mill of an undelighted and servile copulation" at the behest of the canon law. Unhappy marriages are *not* made in heaven, and marital unhappiness destroys peace and affection and thus makes impossible the spiritual development of the persons enslaved by it. Under such conditions, "he who . . . seeks to part is one who highly honors the married life, and would not stain it," and indeed there is one passage in which Milton sees the separation of unmeet consorts as something quite as fundamental as the separation of the world from chaos effected by God himself.

And here again there are flashes from time to time of hardheaded common sense. "The soberest and best governed men" are the likeliest of all to be taken in by an unstable mate, "and who knows not that the bashful muteness of a virgin may often hide all the unliveliness and natural sloth which is really unfit for conversation?" If you admit only adultery as a cause for divorce you will get either feigned or deliberately committed adultery for the purpose of providing grounds for divorce. But Milton goes further still. He knew that a "good" wife may, in fact, wrong her husband even more deeply than an adulteress, for in adultery "nothing is given from the husband which he misses, or enjoys the less." What is more, he knew that even unchastity does not automatically vitiate all good or womanly qualities. "Adultery does not exclude her other fitness, her other pleasingness; she may be otherwise loving and prevalent."

It is true that Milton generally considers the marriage problem from the man's point of view; when he was commenting upon the Scripture passages, which handle only this aspect, there was nothing else he could do. When he sympathizes with the man denied liberty in the senate or the forum because he "languishes under the vilest servitude to an inferior at home," we are likely to retort, "Suppose he serves a *superior?*" But Milton has anticipated us even here, for he knew that this could occur and specifically allows for it:

Not but that particular exceptions may have place, if she exceed her husband in prudence and dexterity, and he contentedly yield; for then a superior and more natural law comes in, that the wiser should govern the less wise, whether male or female.

Though that "and he contentedly yield" might seem to vitiate the qualification, Milton did give women substantially the same rights as men, which was both daring and generous at the time. Finally, and this seems to me most significant of all, he was sensitive enough to realize that bad as it is for a woman to be set aside without cause, she is in even a worse position when she is compelled by church and state to continue to live with a man who does not love her.

V

Whatever else may be said, then, about Milton's attitude toward women, it is surely not unreasonable to urge that the time has finally come when whoever applies the term "misogynist" to him simply knows not whereof he speaks. *Paradise Lost* and *Samson Agonistes* are obviously the poetic works in which he is most concerned with women, and it is equally obvious that both Eve and Dalila behave badly (though Eve also behaves very well), and even Dalila is not so bad as she might very easily have been made. She is Samson's wife, not, as she seems to be in the Bible, his harlot,[22] and though her husband now hates her, he does not behave like Adam after the Fall:

> "This woman whom thou mad'st to be my help,
> And gav'st me as thy perfect gift, so good,
> So fit, so acceptable, so divine,
> That from her hand I could suspect no ill,
> And what she did, whatever in itself,
> Her doing seemed to justify the deed;
> She gave me of the tree, and I did eat."

Samson blames neither God nor man for his fall but takes the

[22] In l. 537, however, Dalila is called Samson's concubine.

127

responsibility squarely upon his own shoulders. He was to blame even for what came through her, for it was his own weakness that gave her power over him. In view of the familiarity with the Samson and Dalila tradition which Milton probably assumed on the part of his readers, it is unlikely that he expected his readers to be taken in by Dalila's defence of herself to the extent that she has succeeded with William Empson,[23] but he did allow her, as Shakespeare allowed Shylock, to state her case, and he certainly made her much less repulsive than she might have been made. Actually there are only two passages—one in *Paradise Lost* and one in *Samson Agonistes*—[24] that express what could in any sense be called misogynist sentiments, and both of these are couched in terms of the conventional denunciation of women in satirical writing, going back to the Middle Ages and, through them, to antiquity, and what is more, both are wholly explicable in terms of both Milton's sources and the situations in hand.

We could afford to give up Dalila if we had to; Eve is the one who counts. Milton had no original in Genesis for his characterization of her. She was female; she was naked; she was tempted; she ate and gave her husband to eat. The rest was his—and tradition's. And whatever Adam may think—or wish to think—Milton has Michael tell us that the real cause of the Fall was not Eve but "man's effeminate slackness." At the close of *Paradise Lost* she is kindly remembered and given the key role in redemption:

"Let her with thee partake what thou hast heard,
Chiefly what may concern her faith to know,

[23] Empson's "A Defence of Dalilah" is in *SR*, LXVIII (1960), 24–55. See also his book, *Milton's God* (CW, 1961), a curiosity of criticism which uses Milton as a stick to beat Christianity with. A much more scholarly and valuable study is that of Mary Ann Nevins Radzinowicz, "Eve and Dalila: Renovation and the Hardening of the Heart," in J. A. Mazzeo, ed., *Reason and the Imagination; Studies in the History of Ideas, 1600–1900* (ColUP, 1962). For the tradition, see again Krouse: "The readers for whom Milton wrote probably reacted to Dalila as they reacted to Satan or Belial: they were prepared for a Devil equipped with what appear on the surface to be the best of arguments. And it must have seemed especially fitting to Protestant Englishmen in the seventeenth century to find the Devil in the person of Dalila citing a prominent Popish commentator for his purpose."
[24] *Paradise Lost*, X, 867 ff.; *Samson Agonistes*, ll. 748 ff.

The great deliverance by her seed to come
(For by the Woman's Seed) on all mankind."

Not that there is any minimizing the wickedness of her sin. Pride, levity, triviality of mind, a sense of "injured merit," stupidity, presumption, frivolity, willfulness, vanity—all this and more has been reasonably found in her. Satan begins his assault upon her mind by planting the idea of God's unreasonableness when he pretends to suppose that all the trees in the Garden have been forbidden her. After she has explained this point to him, he argues that it is safe to disobey God, even beneficial (he is a very modern devil at this point!) and that God himself will approve of her disobedience. Look at me, he says. Before I ate the fruit, I was an ordinary snake; now here I am conversing with you! He lies, of course, and no matter that one argument cancels out another, for being incapable of straight thinking, he always works both sides of the street together, even when he is addressing his committed followers in hell and at last even in his private meditations. But how interesting it is that all even he can ask her to look at is a snake which has become a snake-cum-devil; he cannot show her the archangel who has turned into a devil and, for the time being, into a snake!

Eve is invited to recharacter God according to her own—or, rather, according to Satan's—ideas. For Satan is the tyrant of the Miltonic poetic world, and for all his demagogic talk about freedom, there is no liberty of thought or action while he is by. She is invited to idol-worship, self-worship, and the deification of nature. She resists her first impulse—to conceal her transgression from Adam so that she may establish power over him—but her reason for sharing with him is even more disgraceful than such withholding would have been.

"This may be well. But what if God have seen,
And death ensue? Then I shall be no more,
And Adam wedded to another Eve
Shall live with her enjoying, I extinct;

A death to think. Confirmed then I resolve,
Adam shall share with me in bliss or woe."[25]

Yet it is clear from more than his enamored presentation of her beauty that Milton loved Eve, and if Adam is more intelligent than she is, he is, for that very reason, also more culpable, for she is, in a sense, deceived, while he sins with his eyes open.[26] Milton was no such fool as to try to run with the hares and hunt with the hounds together; having given the woman less than the man, he would not require more from her, though quite enough have attempted just this since his time. He might easily have convicted her of narcissism when she falls in love with her own "smooth watery image," but he avoids this by making her ignorant whom she admires; consequently, she is no more guilty than Adam is when he joys in his own body, which is to say that she is not guilty at all, and if we smile at her, we smile tenderly, as at a small child who quite innocently does something which would be either culpable or embarrassing in a person come to years of discretion. So it is too with her dream of temptation, which might easily have been used to establish her propensity to sin, but Milton has Satan put it into her mind for his own purposes, and

"Evil into the mind of God or man
May come and go, so unapproved, and leave
No spot or blame behind."[27]

[25] I agree with Tillyard ("The Crisis of *Paradise Lost*," in *Studies in Milton*) that there is a comic side to Eve's meditations after eating the apple, and felt this long before reading what he has to say on the subject, but this does not make her less wicked or prove Lewis wrong when he accuses her, in this passage, of contemplating murder.

[26] "Certainly his decision is definite and unhesitating and has been taken without the least pressure from Eve."—Tillyard, "The Crisis of *Paradise Lost*." John S. Diekhoff, *Milton's* Paradise Lost; *A Commentary on the Argument* (ColUP, 1946), perceptively adds that "to be deceived by the deceiver of angels is hardly proof of 'trivial mentality.'"

[27] Murray W. Bundy, "Eve's Dream and the Temptation in *Paradise Lost*," *Research Studies of the State College of Washington*, X (1942), 273–91, expounds this incident in the light of seventeenth-century dream psychology, while William B. Hunter, Jr., "Eve's Demonic Dream," *ELH*, XIII (1946), 255–65, sees it as in line with the more conservative views of the time on the subject of demonology.

In the temptation scene itself, Milton goes out of his way to insist that up to the moment she eats the apple Eve is "yet sinless." It is all very much like *Othello*, where the hero is free of jealousy and all predisposition to jealousy up to the moment when Iago goes to work upon him, yet immediately falls into the tempter's snare. And if, in either case, "psychology" gets in the way of either dramatic effect or the moral lesson, then so much the worse for psychology!

But it is *after* the Fall that we draw closest to Eve. All through history men have been making messes and then going off to leave them. Women sometimes make messes too, but when they do, they are far more likely to stay to clean up after, and often they clean up the man's mess too. It is rarely all or nothing with a woman. She is much more likely to make the best deal that can be made under the circumstances and try to save whatever can be saved out of the wreck. Even when she was inclined to be foolish or rebellious, Eve had always had great dignity.[28] When she and Adam gorge themselves in Book IX and turn from gluttony to lust and from lust to bickering, they are equally unattractive, but she recovers her balance sooner than he does, and it is at least a reasonable question whether he would have been able to make his way back to where we stand now without her to show him the way. He calls her a "serpent" and a "rib crooked by nature" and orders her out of his sight, but she cries,

> "While yet we live, scarce one short hour perhaps,
> Between us two let there be peace"

and

> "Both have sinned, but thou
> Against God only, I against God and thee."

"Only after he has listened to Eve's prayer," says Kester Svendsen

---

[28] Cf., in *Paradise Lost*, II, 270–72:
> To whom the virgin majesty of Eve,
> As one who loves, and some unkindness meets,
> With sweet austere composure thus replied. . . .

finely, "does he realize that God will listen to his."[29] Before he can achieve such peace as is still possible for him, he must receive her as his partner in guilt, not merely Satan's partner in temptation.

[29] "Adam's Soliloquy in Book X of *Paradise Lost*," CE, X (1949), 366–70. The suggestion of racial and personal suicide as a means of avoiding God's doom occurs also in Grotius' *Adamus Exul* (1601), often called a source of *Paradise Lost*. Grotius has the suggestion made by Adam and repudiated by Eve; Milton reverses their respective roles. Since men are somewhat more inclined to self-destruction than women, and since woman's particular job is to carry on the race, Grotius would seem to have the edge here, but this must have contradicted Milton's conviction of male superiority.

IV

MILTON AND CHRIST
AND GOD

I

Since 1825, when *De Doctrina Christiana* was first published, the consideration of Milton's religion has generally begun with his heresies. Parker calls him "a unique combination of semi-Arian, Arminian, Anabaptist, anti-Sabbatarian, Mortalist, semi-Quaker, 'Divorcer,' and polygamist" and adds that he embraced enough heresies to inspire a new catalogue by a Pagitt or an Edwards. His most important heresies are his monism and his rejection of orthodox Trinitarianism, but in dealing with his theology here, we must remember that our interest in this book is the study of his character and personality and not the consideration of his religious "views" for their own sake. Thus, for example, the fact that his monism made it impossible for him to embrace the ascetic point of view is more significant than any strictly philosophical considerations involved in the belief itself.

Milton differed from most Christians in making no clear-cut distinction between matter and spirit. Matter is a coarsened form of spirit, or spirit a refined form of matter, and the Great Chain

133

of Being moved from the grossest to the most ethereal form of the stuff of life itself. "Spirit, being the most excellent substance, virtually and eminently contains within itself the inferior substance." God's omnipresence fills "land, sea, and air and every kind that lives," and other wills can operate only when He "retires" and does not "put forth" his goodness. Since God is infinite, nothing can exist "which had not first been of God and in God." This makes original matter an efflux of the Deity and not something "to be looked upon as an evil or trivial thing, but as intrinsically good, and the chief productive stock of every subsequent good," from which it must follow that God did not create the world out of nothing, which is the orthodox view, but out of himself, a heresy which Calvin specifically repudiates in the *Institutes*.[1]

Consequently Milton could not distinguish between "soul" and "body" in man. For him, man is a unified being, who is born and who dies as one. It would not be correct to say that soul and body die "together" in Milton, for this would imply that they are separate, and for him they are one. The dropping out from Protestant belief of the intermediate state of Purgatory which Catholicism had provided, had caused a good deal of speculation concerning the abiding place of human souls between physical death and the Resurrection of the Last Day. Most Calvinists seem to have believed that redeemed souls went at once to Heaven, there awaiting the Day of Resurrection, when they would be reunited with their bodies. But the Anabaptists and Socinians were "soul sleepers," claiming that this was the early Christian view. It was certainly Milton's view. When a man dies, that is the end of him until the Day of Resurrection, when life will be restored to his unified being.[2]

Milton, I say, believed this, but he did not consider it very im-

[1] See Walter Clyde Curry, "Milton's Dual Concept of God," *SP*, XLVII (1950), 190–210, and, more elaborately, his book, *Milton's Ontology, Cosmogony, and Physics* (University of Kentucky Press, 1957).

[2] See George Williamson, "Milton and the Mortalist Heresy," *SP*, XXXII (1935), 553–79, and Nathaniel H. Henry, "Milton and Hobbes: Mortalism and the Intermediate State," *SP*, XLVIII (1951), 234–49.

portant. For him it was one of the "indifferent" things in religion. Consequently, it is not prominent in his writings. His ideas about the Son and his relationship to his Father, he did consider important, yet it was not until after the *Christian Doctrine* had at last been published that anybody realized that they were at all involved in *Paradise Lost*, and even yet the debate goes on as to whether Milton should be called an Arian or something else.[3]

[3] For Milton as an Arian, see Maurice W. Kelley, *The Great Argument: A Study of Milton's* De Doctrina Christiana *as a Gloss upon* Paradise Lost (PUP, 1941). See especially pp. 57–67 for Kelley's discussion of the most extended preceding study: Arthur Sewell, A *Study of Milton's* Christian Doctrine (OUP, 1939). For criticism of Kelley's position, see the works cited in his reply: "Milton's Arianism Again Considered," HTR, LIV (1961), 195–202. Perhaps the most important point made by those who insist Milton was not an Arian is that he thought of the Son as having been begotten of the Father's own substance while Arius thought of him as begotten *ex nihilo*. "This day I have begot" in *Paradise Lost*, V, 603, may well mean anointed or exalted or elevated or crowned rather than generated, but the case for Milton's anti-Trinitarianism does not rest upon this passage alone. Ruth Montgomery Kivette, who did a doctoral dissertation, "Milton on the Trinity," for Columbia in 1960, thinks him more properly to be called a "subordinationist," and this is accepted by Marjorie Nicolson, *Reader's Guide*, p. 220. The differences between these particular terms may not seem very important to non-theologically minded readers, but even they should be on guard against the sloppy thinkers who would have them believe that Milton was, in any sense in which the term is used now, a "Unitarian." His Christ is about as far from being a "mere man" as it is possible for human thought to go, and it is difficult to see how any theology could make him more important, or assign more important functions to him than Milton does. Christ's using human means to overcome Satan in *Paradise Regained* does not, as some writers have argued, necessarily indicate any lack on Milton's part of faith in his Divinity at the time this poem was written. Christ is tempted in his human aspect, "in all points like as we are, yet without sin." For this reason, too, He must be subjected to temptations which could not possibly have appealed to him personally. They *do* appeal to humanity, and as our Great Elder Brother He must face them and conquer them. Unless He won by use of the only weapons humanity can wield, his example could not greatly benefit us. It is interesting that, though some Renaissance commentators have him tempted "by His own corruption," Milton does not. When his triumph is complete, angels acclaim him quite as He was acclaimed in *Paradise Lost* itself:

"of all creation first,
Begotten Son, Divine Similitude."

Parenthetically it may be remarked that Joseph Moody McDill, *Milton and the Pattern of Calvinism*, Ph.D. thesis, Vanderbilt University, 1942 (Privately printed by The Joint University Libraries, Nashville, Tenn.), probably stands alone in seeing the later Milton as a Calvinist, though Tillyard emphasizes his Puritanism in "Milton and Protestantism" (*The Miltonic Setting*), as does Stoll in the study already cited. It may also be well to add that if Milton is heterodox about the Son, he is even more heterodox about the Holy Spirit, whom he considered "inferior

Basically this was not because Milton was trying to hedge. Art was not a cathartic for him, like the Lawrencian "art for my sake"; he did not even write *Paradise Lost* primarily to express his own religious experience. The poem was an epic, not in the old, traditional, national, or tribal sense, but rather as it involved the fate of the whole human race. Instead of making a personal confession, Milton was creating an epic for the Christian world, and he succeeded so well that for 150 years *Paradise Lost* lay beside the Bible on the center table in tens of thousands of English and American homes without anybody having suspected that there was any conflict or disagreement between the teaching of the two books. Perhaps, after all, there was none. That was what Milton would have said, and that was what he desired.

II

Milton saw Christ as having existed from before the world was made, but not from Eternity. If Christ were coessential with the Father, the term Son would be meaningless in its application to him. The Father begot him in time, of his own volition (it was not *necessary* that He should do so), imparting to him as much of the Divine Substance as He pleased, and being careful not to confound the Substance with the Essence. Though the glory of the Father was "substantially expressed" in Christ, Milton specifically denies that he "knows all things absolutely." One might perhaps say that in his theology the relationship between God and Christ was like the relationship between the ocean and the bay. The bay holds ocean water; in that sense it *is* ocean, but it does not embrace the ocean, it is not all the ocean there is, and ocean cannot be comprehended in bay-terms alone.

to both Father and Son, inasmuch as he is represented and declared to be subservient and obedient in all things; to have been promised and sent, and given; to speak nothing of himself; and even to have been given as an earnest." Milton's problem here was that he based his entire theology upon the Bible, and he found the Bible silent "with regard to the nature of the Holy Spirit, in what manner it exists, or whence it arose." Troubled also by the use of the term "spirit" with other meanings in the Scriptures, he waited to be shown "on what grounds, and by what arguments, we are constrained to believe that the Holy Spirit is God, if Scripture nowhere expressly teach the doctrine of his divinity."

Milton believed in the Incarnation: "God of his own will created, or generated, or produced the Son before all things, endued with the divine nature, as in the fulness of time he miraculously begat him in his human nature of the Virgin Mary."[4] Though he is more orthodox in the Nativity ode and "The Passion" and some of the early pamphlets than he afterwards became, Christ is "Our Savior" and "a virgin is his mother" as late as *Paradise Lost*. He believed in the Atonement too (and the Second Coming also), though as time went on, he seems to have felt that it was "better . . . for us to know simply that the Son of God, our Mediator, was made flesh, that he is called both God and Man, and is such in reality" than it was to be able to explain the matter in formal terms. The third book of *Paradise Lost* is as legalistic as the "governmental" theory of Grotius (whose *Adamus Exul* may have been one of the sources of *Paradise Lost*), but Michael's much warmer discussion in Book XII sounds more like what we now call the "moral influence" theory, which is usually traced back to Abelard but which received its classical form in the work of the nineteenth-century Hartford theologian, Horace Bushnell.[5] As far as it goes, Milton's early poem on "The Passion" seems mechanical and uninspired compared to the Nativity ode; Milton himself gave it up, "finding the subject to be above the years he had, when he wrote it." His choice of the Temptation rather than the Crucifixion as the subject of *Paradise Regained* has usually been attributed to his tendency to stress reason rather than emotion in religion, but his temperamental optimism may have been another factor and his tendency to shy away from physical horror. Moreover, as Douglas Bush has observed, the story of the Crucifixion "had been unapproachably told in the Gospels, and the preparatory trials in the wilderness showed the second Adam winning

---

[4] See William Hunter, "Milton on the Incarnation: Some More Heresies," *JHI*, XXIX (1960), 349–60.

[5] C. A. Patrides, "Milton and the Protestant Theory of the Atonement," *PMLA*, LXXIV (1959), 7–14, studies Milton's views against their historical and contemporary background, effectively demolishing the view that the legalistic element involved was peculiar to him or that it in any way reflects an emphasis peculiarly congenial to his temperament. See further his book, *Milton and the Christian Tradition* (OUP, 1966).

the moral and religious victory over Satan which the first Adam had lost, and exemplifying a kind of heroism within man's reach." If, as is reasonable to suppose, Milton intended a parallel and a contrast between the yielding to a temptation by which mankind was undone in *Paradise Lost* and the conquest over temptation which was a condition of its redemption, then it is difficult to see how else he could have chosen.[6]

It is difficult also to see how Milton could have exalted Christ more than he did, no matter how orthodox his theology might have been. In spite of the first chapter of John ("All things were made by him; and without him was not any thing made that was made"), I doubt that many Christians think of the Son as the Creator. Milton did, though of course he also thought of him as functioning by the power of that divinity whose source is the Father.[7] In the War in Heaven, it is Christ, not Michael, who conquers Satan. He, not the Father, comes to the Garden to pronounce judgment upon Adam and Eve, and it is He who, at the end of all things, will judge us all. Accepting his offer to sacrifice himself to save mankind, the Father says:

"Therefore thy humiliation shall exalt
With thee thy manhood also to this throne;
Here shalt thou sit incarnate, here shalt reign
Both God and man, Son both of God and man,
Anointed universal King."

And, finally, He is, as He was for Whichcote, a kind of Inner Light, "the principle of a divine life within us, as well as a Saviour without us."[8]

The courtly writers of the Middle Ages and the Renaissance

[6] It is interesting to note that Henry Ward Beecher, as he once told Lyman Abbott, preached on virtually every incident in the life of Christ except the Crucifixion. The reason he gave for not preaching on the Crucifixion was that he did not believe he could control his emotions if he were to try. See Abbott, *My Four Anchors* (Pilgrim Press, 1911), p. 14.

[7] For a good summary of various interpretations of Milton's conception of the processes of creation, see Hughes, *Complete Poems and Major Prose*, p. 193.

[8] Cf. Warner G. Rice, *"Paradise Regained," Papers of the Michigan Academy of Science, Arts and Letters*, XXII (1937), 493–503.

often made the point that Christ was the perfect gentleman. I do not know where this could be better illustrated in literature than in Christ's words in Book X, as he goes to pronounce judgment in Eden:

"Father Eternal, thine is to decree,
Mine both in heav'n and earth to do thy will
Supreme, that thou in me thy Son beloved
May'st ever rest well pleased. I go to judge
On earth these thy transgressors; but thou know'st,
Whoever judged, the worst on me must light,
When time shall be; for so I undertook
Before thee, and not repenting, this obtain
Of right, that I may mitigate their doom
On me derived; yet I shall temper so
Justice with mercy as may illustrate most
Them fully satisfied, and thee appease.
Attendance none shall need, nor train, where none
Are to behold the judgment but the judged,
Those two. . . ." [Italics mine.]

When God's children suffer degradation, they have no need of witnesses![9]

Many who would grant all this go on, however, to declare that

---

[9] It would have been strange indeed if any religious-minded pupil of St. Paul's School had not thought about Christ in an intimate and reverential manner. The school was dedicated to the Boy Jesus. The statue of him over the headmaster's chair in the aspect of a teacher, which was saluted with a hymn as the pupils marched in and out, seems to have disappeared by Milton's time, but the influence must have lingered, and the Monday afternoon prayer summed up its meaning:

Our Lord and Master, Sweetest Jesus, who while yet a boy of twelve years, disputed in such manner among those doctors in the temple at Jerusalem that all were amazed at thy most excellent wisdom, we ask thee that in this thy school, of which thou art head and patron, we may know thee, Jesus, who art the true wisdom, then out of that knowledge worship and be like thee, and in this short life walk in the way of thy teaching, so following thy steps that, as thou thyself hast attained, we descending out of this light, may also blessedly attain some portion of His glory through thy grace.

In view of these facts, Hanford's conjecture that Milton may have experienced a "conversion" at St. Paul's School is quite in order, though one may doubt that he ever thought of it quite in modern evangelistic terms.

if Milton's Christ is a gentleman, his God is not; this view seems based upon a misapprehension. It is the Son who offers to die for man, but it is the Father who accepts the sacrifice because it is harmony with his will that mercy should "colleague with justice." God's *permissive* will was involved in allowing man to fall (man can neither be lost nor saved without his own choice being involved in the process), but his *active* will is involved in redemption, so that there is no conflict between him and the Son at any point. The fact that Christ appears as the warrior who conquers Satan also undercuts the notions of those who would overemphasize the contrast between the stern Father and the loving Son.

In other words, when, as Pope said, Milton made God reason like a school divine, both he and his God were victims of his method. He knew as well as we do that to present the Infinite in a work of art is to attempt the impossible, this being an area where one cannot hope for success but must settle for relative degrees of failure, and this is not the only place in *Paradise Lost*, where, as Irene Samuel reminds us, we need to learn to distinguish between dogma and drama.[10] The problem is easier with the Son because He is thought of as having lived a human life as Jesus of Nazareth, but even here it can be troublesome; how many pictures of Christ can you think of which do not degrade your conception of him? Whatever Milton's theology, he could not have written the third book of *Paradise Lost* without presenting Father and Son as distinct personae and allowing each to express his own point of view. God must explain himself, justify himself, and deliver lectures on theology, and Milton surely knew as well as we do that, realistically considered, all this is not only unthinkable but even undignified or embarrassing. There may even be moments when we are tempted to believe that Robert Nathan found a better way when he had God declare, in his *Jonah*, that "actually at the moment I am not interested in theology"! We simply have to be sophisticated enough to make allowance for epic needs and con-

10 "The Dialogue in Heaven: A Reconsideration of *Paradise Lost*, III, 1–147," PMLA, LXXII (1957), 601–22, reprinted in Barker, *Milton: Modern Essays in Criticism*.

ventions and read what the author is trying to say not only through them but around them.

Helen Gardner writes with her usual perspicacity when she remarks that "to think of Milton as conceiving of God as the strategist and ironist of his poem is as naïve as to think of Michelangelo as believing that God possessed a pair of powerful legs." But not even great Milton scholars have always been so astute; thus we find Sir Herbert Grierson saying that Milton's heaven is a totalitarian state. It is nothing of the kind, for Milton did not believe that God was free to do what He would or that his mere will was supreme; reason must rule in God as well as man, and no rational being can reconcile contradictions. God is not free to do wrong, for example; He cannot make the mortal immortal nor the finite infinite. As Lyman Abbott once put it, "The Ten Commandments are not right because God commanded them; God commanded them because they were right." By the same token, a man who walks off a precipice does not break the law of gravitation but merely illustrates it. In other words, Milton agreed with Whichcote that "right and just are determined, not by the arbitrary pleasure of him that has power over us; but by the nature and reason of things." To do the will of God, consequently, is to be free, living in harmony with him, with one's own nature, and with the constitution of the world that God made. There is only one tyrant in *Paradise Lost,* and his name is Satan.

Milton's kindly conception of the character of God is shown also in his rejection of total depravity and his repudiation of the Calvinistic doctrine of foreordination and election. Though he did not believe in universal salvation, Milton obviously tried to make it as difficult as possible to be damned. "For God has predestinated to salvation, on the proviso of a general condition, all who enjoy freedom of will; while none are predestinated to destruction, except through their own fault." Though grace is not given to all in equal measure, all have sufficient for salvation, and "reprobation is rescinded by repentance." Men are judged by their own knowledge and conscience and those to whom Christ has not been revealed may be saved through faith in God alone. None are excluded "unless it be after the contempt and rejection of grace, and that at a very late hour."[11]

III

Was Milton, then, a champion of religious freedom, as we understand the term? The answer must be qualified. Both in his attitude toward the Bible and in his attitude toward the church he achieves a combination of freedom and authoritarianism, or of mediaevalism and modernism, which is all his own.

Milton's first pamphlets were not hostile to episcopacy, and we must remember that he himself originally intended to be a clergyman. His own statement that he was "church-outed" by the prelates seems to have been true only in the sense that his own increasing dissatisfaction with the church as England drew closer to civil war created conscientious scruples for him; there is no record of the church having taken action against him. Though St. Paul's School exposed him to the religious power of the cathedral service and all that goes with it, he was to become increasingly indifferent to the sacramental conception of religion as he grew older. In rejecting all the sacraments except baptism and the Lord's Supper, he was merely Protestant, but he regarded neither as indispensable (he rejected both Catholic transubstantiation and Lutheran consubstantiation and taught that baptism, if practiced at all, must be administered only to adults and in running water), nor was a clergyman required to administer them. He opposed tithing as belonging to the Law, not the Gospel; the same was true of Sabbath-keeping, and he could find no Scriptural authority for making Sunday a Christian holy day. He did not take much stock in ordination anyway, being unable to perceive that it produced any beneficial change in the character of the "hirelings" who submitted themselves to it, of whose deficiencies, as all the world knows, he was painfully aware as early as "Lycidas." He once called most clergymen bunglers who would have starved to death in business. It is true that the fact that there are unfaithful

[11] See Maurice Kelley, "The Theological Dogma of *Paradise Lost,* III, 173–202," *PMLA,* LII (1937), 75–79.

shepherds would have been a poor excuse for Milton's failure to give the church a good one in the person of himself, and, like Emerson (though in his case not until *after* ordination), he seems less to have repudiated the idea than to have outgrown it. His dislike of public speaking may have contributed—he once said that he hardly ever spoke in public of his own volition—and his later conception of *all* talents and gifts being dedicated to God opened up the way for him to serve God upon a larger stage than any pulpit could supply.[12]

Ecclesiastically speaking, Milton's own religious progress was, as Hanford has put it, "through Presbyterianism to Independency and finally to pure individualism." When Presbyterianism grew authoritarian, he deserted it for Independency, and when, in 1652, there seemed a danger of turning Independency itself into Establishment, he addressed one of his noblest sonnets to "Cromwell, our chief of men" in protest:

> peace hath her victories
> No less renowned than war; new foes arise
> Threat'ning to bind our souls with secular chains.
> Help us to save free conscience from the paw
> Of hireling wolves whose gospel is their maw.

Milton gravitated toward personal freedom through his insistence that faith can only be based on individual religious experience and study of the Scriptures and that no mediator can stand between the soul and God. To interfere with this would be like

---

[12] Milton gave considerable thought to the economic aspects of a hired ministry, rightly seeing a great source of corruption here (it must be remembered that he lived in a time and a country in which "livings" were often given to men who had no "vocation" but had turned to the church as other men turn to other forms of earning their livelihood. The only way to avoid this danger altogether would be to establish an unsalaried clergy who should serve for love and support themselves by some other occupation carried on simultaneously, but Milton knew that this was not practicable and that some compromise must therefore be accepted. One of the most puzzling aspects of his thinking in this area is that he tended to think the clergy should not concern themselves with civic affairs. Since he regarded his own life and career as a ministry, one wonders how he reconciled this with his own conduct.

trying to yoke the Holy Spirit himself. Adam and Eve observe not rites

> but adoration pure,
> Which God likes best,

and Milton himself finally rebelled against all set forms, even stated or prescribed times of prayer. Instead of being frightened by the multiplicity of sects and schisms he witnessed during his later years, he regarded them as signs of renewed vitality; an established church, he granted, could prevent schism but only at the cost of producing "numb and chill stupidity" of soul and "inactive blindness" of mind. He himself did not attend any church during his last years, and in September, 1664, he was in trouble for violating the Conventicle Act. If he never went as far as Roger Williams in opting for religious liberty (we have elsewhere glanced at the grounds on which he refuses toleration to Catholics), he did come to sympathize strongly with Protestant ecumenicalism.

The Bible, for Milton, was God's Word, the fount of all religious truth and the supreme authority in all questions involving religion. Church councils had no authority in his eyes, for even the primitive church was corrupt. His own direct study of the Bible was the basis of his *Christian Doctrine* ("for my own part, I adhere to the Holy Scriptures alone—I follow no other heresy or sect");[13] everything that contradicted the Bible was heresy, and there was no other heresy. "Let us then discard reason in sacred matters, and follow the doctrine of Holy Scripture exclusively." In 1656 he refused to be greatly moved by Henry Oldenburg's interest in the forthcoming "ancient annals of the Chinese from the Flood downwards"; he could see the interest attaching to "the novelty of the thing," but he could not "see what authority or confirmation they can add to the Mosaic books." Yet, as we shall see, Milton's own interpretation of the Bible was highly specialized and extremely Miltonic. As Tillyard pointed out, he had little

---

[13] See, however, Maurice Kelley, "Milton's Debt to Wolleb's *Compendium Theologiae Christianae*," PMLA, L (1935), 156–65.

interest in the Biblical miracles. Since they were in the Bible, he could not leave them out of his *Christian Doctrine*, but he reduces his treatment of them to about half a page.

In his conception of religious authority as lodged in an infallible book, Milton is "fundamentalist" rather than "modern," but his practice came much closer to modernism than anyone might have expected with his presuppositions. He sees the Old Covenant as having been definitely superseded by the New, and he makes some allowance for the possibility of textual corruption; otherwise he allows very inadequately for a spiritual evolution within the Bible itself or for the presence of a human factor in it, limiting and conditioning its revelation of the Divine Will.[14] It was upon this basis that he achieved the most revolting and absurd thing in the *Christian Doctrine*, his championship of polygamy on the ground that God had permitted and sanctioned it in the days of the patriarchs, and these holy men must not be stamped as adulterous nor their God himself as condoning adultery!

Moreover, God himself, in an allegorical fiction, Ezek. xxiii, 4. represents himself as having espoused two wives, Aholah and Aholibah; a mode of speaking which he would by no means have employed, especially at such length, even in a parable, nor indeed have taken on himself such a character at all, if the practice which it implied had been intrinsically dishonorable or shameful.[15]

[14] Compare the much more "modern" way in which he approaches the problems involved in early British history, as described by Parker, pp. 338 ff.

[15] Stoll (*Poets and Playwrights*) has a cogent comment here, effectively summing up at least one aspect of Milton's teaching, which happens to be an aspect modern interpreters have been inclined to minimize:

He is nothing at all of a naturalist but a legalist. The one relation, of marriage, is proper and right, and even to the intemperate point of polygamy; the other, beyond the bounds of wedlock, is wholly wrong. It is a matter of obedience, again, not of temperance, of free indulgence in the one case, of total abstinence in the other, not of moderation or excess. The Mormons, we must remember, came of Puritan stock, and were of that tradition; the Mormons, like the Puritans, the ancient Hebrews and the Mohammedans, were legalists, self-indulgent in one regard, strong prohibitionists in others, and exemplars of temperance in none.

On the other hand, Milton quite disdains the "proof-text" method of Biblical interpretation which modern "fundamentalists" employ. He does not regard the citation of this or that particular passage of Scripture as sufficient either to establish or to refute a religious opinion. What he does is to interpret individual passages in terms of general sense and impression as informed by Christian charity, his understanding of the spirit of the Bible as a whole, and his conception of the character of God. This is what he does with divorce, for example, when he calls Christ's prohibition except for adultery an extreme statement, called out by the extreme abuses of the time, and not to be taken literally. "Was our Savior so mild and favorable to the weakness of a single man, and is he turned on the sudden, so rigorous, so inexorable, to the distresses and extremities of an ill-wedded man?" And again: "Whoso prefers either matrimony or other ordinance before the good of man and the plain exigence of charity, let him profess papist or protestant, or what he will, he is no better than a pharisee, and understands not the gospel."

In other words, Milton believed that God intended him to use his brains when he read his Bible—the law of right reason and the law of nature—but he also believed that brains alone would not avail without the guidance and interpretation of the Holy Spirit.

It was also evident to me that, in religion as in other things, the offers of God were all directed, not to an indolent credulity, but to constant diligence and to an unwearied search after truth, and that more than I was aware of still remained which required to be more rigidly examined by the rule of Scripture and reformed after a more accurate model.

Even the purest record could not be understood "but by the Spirit."

When Charles Dickens came to America in 1842, he made for himself the same rule about parading his views on slavery that Milton followed concerning religion when he was in Italy. He never brought the subject up himself, but when it was raised by his hosts (which was often enough to suggest that their minds were not quite at ease about the matter), he would not evade the issue. One slavery advocate asked him whether he believed in the Bible. "Yes, I said, but if any man could prove to me that it sanctioned slavery, I would place no further credence in it." Later he explained what he had meant by this:

It is enough for me to be satisfied, on calm inquiry and with reason, that an Institution or Custom is wrong and bad; and thence to feel assured that *it cannot* be a part of the law laid down by the Divinity who walked the earth. Though every other man who wields a pen should turn himself into a commentator on the Scriptures—not all their united efforts, pursued through our united lives, could ever persuade me that Slavery is a Christian law; nor, with any of these objections to an execution in my certain knowledge, that Executions are a Christian law, my will is not concerned. I could not, in my veneration for the life and lessons of Our Lord, believe it. If any text appeared to justify the claim, I would reject that limited appeal, and rest upon the character of the Redeemer, and the great scheme of his Religion, where, in its broad spirit, made so plain—and not this or that disputed letter—we all put our trust. . . . We know that the law of Moses was delivered to certain wandering tribes, in a peculiar and perfectly different social condition from that which prevails among us at this time. We know that the Christian Dispensation did distinctly repeal and annul certain portions of that law.

Except that he makes less provision for "the law of Moses" having been "delivered to certain wandering tribes, in a peculiar and perfectly different social condition from that which prevails among us at this time," this is about what Milton would have said. But Dickens is franker about his premises and more logical in following them through to their ultimate conclusions; he seems, indeed, more like George Fox than he is like Milton. It is true that in *Paradise Regained* Christ himself declares that

147

"He who receives
Light from above, from the Fountain of Light,
No other doctrine needs, though granted true."

Milton does not often go quite so far as that. But his insistence that religion was personal, not institutional, and that every man must interpret the Bible according to his own understanding rather than that of another helped open up the way to freedom. To say, or to hear another say, that he preferred the Inner Light to the Scriptures would have shocked him; what he did instead was to prove, to his own satisfaction at least, that the Scriptures are in harmony with the Inner Light, and it was inevitable that in doing this, he should sometimes have fallen into what to the twentieth-century mind looks like casuistry. Sometimes he gives the impression of having appealed to reason and then set to work in search of evidence to prove that what he already believed was sanctioned by the Scriptures. As Dora Raymond puts it, "his use of the Bible is . . . to add possible authority to a message he has heard in secret."

Did Milton, then, take his Bible literally? In the sense that he thought the Bible meant what it said, yes. But what it "meant" did not necessarily correspond to objective (if the word can apply in such a connection) "Reality."

Because he preferred to have the Bible read rather than "read into," Milton generally rejects the allegorical approach, though he accepts it in the case of the Song of Solomon, I suppose because only on that basis, rejected by modern scholars, can it have anything more than an erotic meaning.[16] Most of the hexameral poets took the War in Heaven allegorically; Hughes thinks that for Milton it was both allegorical and real. Eden seems to have been a real place to him and to his contemporaries in general. But he could not possibly have expected *Paradise Lost* to be taken literally when he departs from the Scriptures, as in the Sin and Death allegory, and he must have known that neither Belial nor Mammon were proper names in the Bible.

[16] See H. R. MacCallum, "Milton and the Figurative Interpretation of the Bible," *UTQ*, XXXI (1953), 397–415.

While he was still thinking of what finally became *Paradise Lost* as a drama, he considered nearly one hundred subjects for it, but if he wished to "justify the ways of God to men" in terms of the religious thought of his time, it is difficult to see why he needed to consider more than one of them. In some sense, he must, then, have believed in a "Fall." Those for whom Genesis is not history but folklore must now grapple with the problem of evil in other ways, and no end of writers have attempted this, clear on down to H. G. Wells (*The Undying Fire*), Thornton Wilder (*The Bridge of San Luis Rey*), and Archibald MacLeish (*J.B.*). In *Through Nature to God* John Fiske made a pretty good job of justifying evil in terms of the evolutionary philosophy; in *The Problem of God* and other writings, the "Personalist" philosopher, Edgar Sheffield Brightman, saw God as limited by something in the stuff of Creation which He had not yet been able to bring under control. Yet one reason why *Paradise Lost* has lived as a work of art, and as a valid interpretation of human experience, is that it retains meaning even for those for whom the literalistic portion of Milton's presuppositions now seems outmoded. Till-yard touched upon this in the brilliant Epilogue to his *Milton,* where he clearly demonstrated that Milton's attitude toward life has nothing distinctively seventeenth century about it.

Milton saw humanity free, in a way capable of guiding its fate, and with a certain instinct towards virtue; yet subject to a curious levity of disposition or sloth, which prevented most men from taking advantage of their powers. Passion only too often usurped reason's sway, and some sort of enslavement followed. Yet the possibility of self-mastery, of regeneration, remained; and a few prospered in self-betterment. Generally speaking the world could be improved almost indefinitely, but in fact use was not made of the great opportunity. Now whether Milton was right or not, at least his notion has nothing specifically to do with the seventeenth century; it is as applicable today. His notion of the Fall would for some people fit in perfectly with the spectacle of modern humanity equipped with the mechanical power to obtain decent living for all, in a way desirous of using it, and yet apparently incapable of turning this power to account. . . .

In other words, even if we regard him as having achieved it by dubious means, Milton's attitude toward life still has validity. The twentieth century may, if it chooses, banish the word "sin" from our vocabularies, but the state of our insane asylums and mental hospitals will remain to prove that you do not change the nature of human experience by changing its name. Interpret Adam and Eve, and even God himself, if you like, as a set of symbols, and they will still be found adequate to what Milton requires of them—to his aesthetic purpose unquestionably and probably to his moral or theological purpose as well, for we should remember that Milton believed Spenser to be a better teacher than Scotus or Aquinas.

Moreover, though Milton in a sense took his Bible literally, he took it thus in a very specialized sense.[17] Whatever else he disagreed with Calvin about, he accepted his doctrine of accommodation. As Roland M. Frye puts it,[18]

Calvin taught that Scripture does not plainly express what God is, but adapts the understanding of him to human capacity, for while we are in an earthly condition "we need symbols and mirrors to exhibit to us the appearance of spiritual and heavenly things in a kind of earthly way." These symbols do not show us "what God is in himself, but what he is to us" and so "there is no need for the reality to agree at all points with the symbol, if only it suit sufficiently for the purpose of symbolizing." . . . Thus in connection with the final judgment, Calvin treats the apocalyptic symbols in terms of their ultimate meaning, that God will totally conquer all sin and evil, rather than of their

17 For further discussion see E. N. S. Thompson, "The Theme of *Paradise Lost*," PMLA, XXVIII (1913), 106–120; H. W. Peck, "The Theme of *Paradise Lost*," PMLA, XXIX (1914), 256–69; A. H. Gilbert, "The Problem of Evil in Paradise Lost," JEGP, XXII (1923), 175–94.

18 *God, Man, and Satan: Patterns of Christian Thought and Life in* Paradise Lost, Pilgrim's Progress, *and the Great Theologians* (PUP, 1960).

literal content. He therefore interprets the last trumpet as meta-phorical, and writes that "the fact that the stars fall from heaven is not to be understood literally, but as an image adapted to our capacities of understandings."

In other words, God reveals himself by speaking "as it were child-ishly, as nurses do"; to know him as He is transcends the power of man's thought and perception. As we read in *Paradise Lost,*

> "objects divine
> Must needs impair and weary human sense"

and again,

> "Immediate are the acts of God, more swift
> Than time or motion, but to human ears
> Cannot without process of speech be told,
> So told as earthly notion can receive."

Raphael therefore so adapts his explanation of Divinity to Adam that

> "what surmounts the reach
> Of human sense I shall delineate so,
> By lik'ning spiritual to corporeal forms,
> As may express them best."

Man can know God only through his attributes, and of these the Bible gives us only what we can grasp.

Our safest way is to form in our minds such a conception of God as shall correspond with his own delineation and repre-sentation of himself in the sacred writings. For granting that both in the literal and figurative descriptions of God, he is exhibited not as he really is, but in such a manner as may be within the scope of our apprehensions, yet we ought to enter-tain such a conception of him, as he, in condescending to ac-commodate himself to our capacities, has shewn that he desires we should conceive.[19]

[19] Helen Gardner, A *Reading of* Paradise Lost, p. 18.

What this means is that though the Bible is not literally true, we must accept it as if it were, for it expresses all the truth we can grasp, which, practically speaking, means that for us it *is* the truth, We must not take discounts or make allowances in reading it, for God has already done this for us in the sacred text itself, and the Bible as it stands is net.

It may be that Milton's familiarity and consanguinity of temperament with Platonism, which views the world itself as a very imperfect expression of the pure, immaterial Reality which exists in its perfection only beyond this mortal plane, may have helped him to perceive all this. And this brings us to the whole moot matter of Milton's attitude toward pagan learning.

IV

That Milton was himself thoroughly grounded in the classics no student who has ever tried to follow up his references has ever doubted. He himself avows his indebtedness to the Athenian Greeks and declares that "whatever literary advance I have made I owe chiefly to steady intimacy with their writings from my youth upwards." And, as we have already seen, he was not limited to this area; instead his mind roved over the whole field of learning known to his time. I have already spoken of his references to folklore, in "L'Allegro" and elsewhere, and Patricia Merivale has recently found him "the most important single figure in the pre-Romantic development of the Pan motif." After him, English authors had "virtually the whole scale of possible Pan references to draw upon."[20] Long ago, William Vaughn Moody wrote.

Nothing is more remarkable in Milton's handling of the materials of his intellectual world than his persistent linking of classic and pseudo-classic myth with what he conceived to be permanent religious truth. The best known examples of this are to be found in "Lycidas," where St. Peter appears in the same procession with Triton and Father Camus . . . and in the famous

[20] *Pan the Goat-God: His Myth in Modern Times* (HUP, 1969), pp. 28–34.

identification in *Paradise Lost* of the heathen gods with the fallen angels.[21]

Paradise Regained itself is full of classical learning, even in the passages where it is being minimized or repudiated, as when Christ himself is made to praise Socrates.[22]

The repudiation *is* made, however, though it is also qualified, and as it stands it is quite in harmony with Milton's general beliefs. Learned as he was, his attitude toward learning was always strictly pragmatic, as we have already seen, and no man who knew so much ever wore his learning more lightly. He wanted to teach as Christ taught, "as one having authority, and not as the scribes," and he had only scorn for those who can merely quote.

"However, many books,
Wise men have said are wearisome; who reads
Incessantly, and to his reading brings not
A spirit and judgment equal or superior
(And what he brings, what needs he elsewhere seek?),
Uncertain and unsettled still remains,
Deep versed in books and shallow in himself,
Crude or intoxicate, collecting toys
And trifles for choice matters, worth a sponge,
As children gathering pebbles on the shore."

"Pomp and ostentation of reading is admired among the vulgar," he says; "but doubtless in matters of religion he is learnedest who is plainest." To him learning was nourishment for the mind and spirit and not an end in itself (that was part of Eve's mistake):

"But knowledge is as food, and needs no less
Her temperance over appetite, to know
In measure what the mind may well contain,
Oppresses else with surfeit, and soon turns
Wisdom to folly, as nourishment to wind."

[21] This subject has now been much more fully explored than it had been in Moody's time; see, by way of example, the instances cited in Bush's notes, pp. 114, 170, 174, 200, 279, 394.
[22] Note especially the classical comparison in IV, 560 ff.

Nevertheless, Milton does give Hebraic materials the preference over pagan materials and Christian over non-Christian. Readers of the Nativity ode and of *Paradise Lost* will not need to be told how much more severely he treats the "heathen" gods who came in contact with the Jews than he does the others. His invocations in *Paradise Lost*, though classical in form, are essentially Christian prayers in intent, and Milton makes it clear that the reason for this is that only the Christian inspiration can serve for what he is trying to achieve. If it be asked, then, why the non-Christian materials should appear at all, the answer must be that Milton was a Renaissance humanist as well as a Reformation Protestant, and the mingling of Christian and pagan materials was character-istic of all Renaissance culture. He did not get so far as what we call "comparative religion" (in *Paradise Regained* it is advocated by Satan!), but he did see foreshadowings of Christian truths in non-Christian writings, and more directly, of course, as all Chris-tians did, in the Old Testament. Nevertheless, he very carefully protects the reader, and when pagan and Christian stories stand side by side, he often calls the former "feigned" or "fabled."

Essentially the Christian material is superior because it is based upon revelation. Hellenism is not evil in itself, and Hebraism has not so much annihilated as subsumed it. Christ himself is not ignorant of it: "Think not but that I know these things." What Milton does in *Paradise Regained*, then, is not to have Christ reject pagan learning absolutely, as He has rejected other tempta-tions; He simply refuses to exchange it for what He has. "All knowledge is ignorance, except it conduce to the knowledge of the Scriptures," said John Donne, "and all the Scriptures lead us to Christ." It sounds a little like Christ's own attitude toward John the Baptist (he was greatest among the children of men, but the least in the Kingdom was greater than he), and it is difficult to see how anyone who believes that in any sense Christianity stands apart from other religions as bringing a new revelation or introducing a new element into human life, can disagree with Milton upon this count.[23]

23 His avowed preference for David as his favorite poet is puzzling in the light

The same considerations apply to and explain Milton's similar apparent disparagement of the importance of learning for "those laziest of animals," as he calls them, the clergy. Certainly he did not neglect it when he thought he was preparing himself for the ministry. But he would have agreed entirely with the clergyman who, upon being asked whether the things he could not understand in the Bible troubled him, replied, "Not at all. It is the things I *can* understand in the Bible which trouble me." Milton did not believe that the essential Gospel, addressed by God to all mankind, was in itself difficult to apprehend, and he saw a great deal of the intellectual equipment which clergymen think they need as conducing more effectively to intellectual pride than to spiritual grace, and tending rather to "perplex and leaven pure doctrine with scholastic trash than enable any minister to the better preaching of the gospel." Moreover, he refused to equate intellectual accomplishment with spiritual qualifications. The wind bloweth where it listeth. God could ordain without the schools, and were it his good pleasure, He could cause the foolish things of this world to confound the mighty.

Because he based his religion on reason and authority, Milton is commonly denied the capacity for mystical experience. Unlike John Donne, he did not write about his personal religious experience but about universal religious experience; he even overlooked some of the specific religious problems which interested his contemporaries most.[24] All this is the more remarkable with such a self-dramatizing artist as he was, and perhaps needs to be taken into account as putting a brake upon the self-centeredness which some critics find so offensive in him. I have no particular interest in setting up a case for Milton as a mystic, but it does seem to me that he has often been denied this capacity in far too sweeping and all-inclusive terms. He always insists that religion *is* direct experience, and he thought of Christians as living "in the most intimate union" with Christ. He seems to have thought of himself

of his own paraphrases of the Psalms. If we compare these with what Milton achieved in writings inspired by classical epic and drama, it is hard to believe that David moved him very deeply as an artist.

[24] See Gardner, *A Preface to* Paradise Lost.

in this aspect; certainly there can be no question that he conceived of his whole life and all his powers as dedicated to God's work in the world. He saw the operation of the Holy Spirit as vitally important for the salvation of men's souls and the final, infallible guide in Christian ethics, and out of the agony of his blindness he expressed his faith in God's guidance and loving care.[25]

[25] Milton's interest in occultism and the special appeal which the Book of Revelation made to him do not support the assumption of an exclusively legalistic or intellectual approach to religion; see Hanford, *John Milton, Poet and Humanist*, pp. 62–65. For a masterly defence of Milton against his modern critics from the convinced Christian point of view, cf. George Wesley Whiting, *Milton and This Pendant World* (University of Texas Press, 1958).

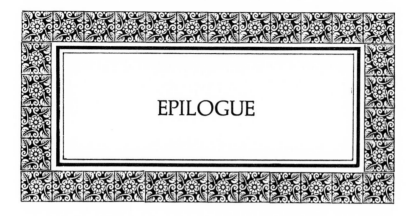

EPILOGUE

We have been entertained (greatly I may say, speaking of myself) with the picture of a man, of a mind, as well worthy our consideration and esteem as most of those whose lives are written by any ancient or modern, more than far the greater number, and the rather as being within the reach in some degree, I mean his piety and virtue, of our imitation. Whatever spots or blemishes appear upon his judgment in certain points, let the charitable eye look beyond those on his immaculate integrity. Such who have not hitherto done this, but have suffered what they have been taught, or chosen to dislike in him, to eclipse him, so that, though they see him to be a great poet, they look on him as shining with a sort of disastrous light, will, if they possess good minds, rejoice in finding a character amiably bright where they expected no such, and will perhaps read him with more delight and enrich their own minds the more by so doing than if themselves had continued laboring under their old prejudices.

Explanatory Notes and Remarks on Milton's
Paradise Lost, by J. Richardson, Father and
Son, With the Life of the Author and a Discourse
on the Poem. By J. R. Sen. London, 1734.

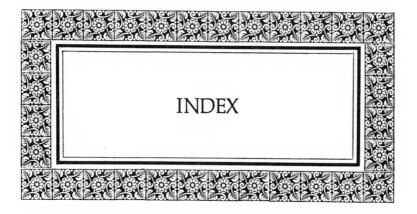

INDEX